A Widow's Walk
Off-Grid to Self-Reliance

An inspiring, true story of
Courage and Determination

Annie Dodds

~ ~ ~

Mason Marshall Press
Medford, Massachusetts

No part of this book may be used, reproduced, stored in or introduced into a retrieval system, or transmitted in any manner by any means, known or unknown, without express written permission from the publisher, except in the case of brief quotations embodied in critical articles and reviews.

Published by Mason Marshall Press

Copyright © 2014 by Anne Dodds
Cover art Copyright © 2014 by Mason Marshall Press.
All rights reserved.

ISBN-13: 978-1-63247-000-3
ISBN-10: 1632470004

For information, please contact:
Mason Marshall Press
P.O. Box 324,
Medford, MA 02155

PRINTED IN THE UNITED STATES OF AMERICA

I hesitated to dedicate this book to any one person for fear of hurting the feelings of so many who have become friends, but there were two who are no longer with us, who stood out to many of us – Preliator, a city dweller, and Melonghunter, a trapper, bow-hunter, and Maine farmer. They meant so much to me and to so many others and their loss has left a gap in many lives.

To them, and to all my friends whose words, advice, encouragement, and help meant so much to me in my dark days, thank you.

You will all live in my heart forever.

Publisher's Note

The story you are about to read is true.

It was first written in chunks, more as a stream-of-consciousness remembrance than a narrative. While the author and editor worked hard to transform the original thoughts into the inspiring story that follows, they did so trying to retain as much as possible of the original structure and flavor. Each "chunk" is separated by ~ ~ ~ except for a few spots at the beginning and end.

Prologue

I thought about writing this for a very long time. I kept asking myself how I could write about something so real and raw – about a time when I was left broke to fend for myself, still reeling from my husband's death.

This isn't a story about how great I am, or was. It isn't about all the things I discovered how to do. It's about learning how to grieve and still live. It's about learning it's possible to survive, alone and un-prepared, something I never imagined I would ever have to do. It's about learning to walk a path that would teach me how to recover my life.

I always felt a kinship with the country and the backwoods and admired the pioneer life, the spirit of doing whatever is necessary to survive. When I married and started a family, little did I know that one day I would have to become one of those pioneers, with only my wits and a thirst for learning to keep me going.

This is my story.

Please join me on my widow's walk off-grid, to self-reliance.

Annie Dodds

The Early Years

I met Jim at a meeting in Corpus Christi, Texas, where we both lived. I had been attending the 12-step program on my road to recovery from alcoholism. Jim was a veteran and a recovering alcoholic working in the field as a counselor. We liked each other right away and began to see each other socially, which, in the beginning, mainly meant going to meetings together. We married late in 1985.

My three boys were mostly grown and off doing their own thing. My then twelve-year-old daughter lived with her dad by mutual agreement, but after a while, as my recovery progressed and my life stabilized again, she would come to live with us.

Jim and I had no children together and he had been estranged from his two grown sons for many years.

Jim was a dedicated counselor and as my recovery progressed, I began to unofficially assist him, which taught me a valuable lesson – that sometimes, the best way to help ourselves is to help others. He often handled the people who were court referrals; people who tended to be the saddest and most downtrodden. Caught up in their addiction, they seemed helpless and hopeless. We spent many hours, many days working with those who suffered most from their addictions. It was a very different world than I had ever known, one I never again wanted to allow myself to live in.

The Good Times Go Bad
1993-1995

Life was good. We loved each other and the years slid by. Then, in 1993, Jim developed an aggravating little cough. Since he was due for his thyroid test, I encouraged him to tell the doctor about it. The doctor scheduled him for an MRI which found a mass in his chest. He was immediately scheduled for testing and a biopsy.

Two weeks later, Jim and I traveled to the veterans' hospital at Ft. Sam Houston in San Antonio for his work up. It would be a long day of invasive tests and the doctors told me it would be quite a while before they were through, that I should go eat, but food was never even a thought. My mind went on lock-down, so I got in the car and drove to the PX – the on-base store – to pick up a few things.

As I passed the magazine rack, I caught a glimpse of a magazine with a cabin, set in the woods in the snow, on the cover. The name was *Backwoods Home*. I picked it up and remember looking at that cabin thinking someday I would live a relaxed country life, the kind of life I once wanted, but had put on hold, because our dreams are not always the dreams of those we love. I laugh now at the thoughts I had of a glamorous, relaxed country life. I didn't know it, but I was in for a big surprise. Life wouldn't be glamorous. Just the opposite. But it would teach me more than I could ever have imagined.

I did my shopping and drove back to the hospital. As I entered the cancer ward, they were bringing Jim out of the surgical area. The doctor, who we came to respect and love, looked at me, shook his head, and looked away. Looking back, I guess that moment was, for me, the beginning of the end.

The next morning, when Jim was released from the ward, we had an appointment with the doctor. Military doctors are different than civilians. They don't hem and haw or talk about the weather. They generally come straight to the point and this one was no different. He gave us the heart stopping, gut slamming painful news – Jim had nine months to a year to live.

He gave us an option to participate in a trial of a new chemotherapy drug. Jim looked at me. He knew I would back him all the way and reading each other's minds like married people do, he turned back to the doctor and said, "Let's do it."

Two weeks later, we began a series of six chemo treatments. After the third week, the doctors were very excited – the cancer had shrunk 65%. We were beyond happy.

About three weeks later, I received a call at work to go home because Jim was in serious physical distress. I raced home and called the oncology doctor. He said bring him immediately so I bundled him up and drove as fast as I dared. Two days of testing later, they gave me the horrible news that Jim was in kidney failure. They had to suspend the chemotherapy. The doctor, too, was devastated, despite knowing the chemo worked. He would later say Jim had provided hope for thousands and they could move forward with more tests on other cancer patients.

The doctor and I agreed not to tell Jim just then. We needed to get him stable and calm and I needed time to digest this second death sentence.

~ ~ ~

The morning they released him, we walked down to the little coffee shop in the basement of the hospital while we waited for his prescriptions to be filled. He was on a no-caffeine diet, so he got a root-beer and I had a coffee. They sold so much coffee in that little basement shop, it was always fresh and I needed fresh. Lots of it.

We walked outside and sat on the steps. Jim still didn't know how bad things were, but I think he suspected, because we sat there, together, in a stunned silence until a sparrow lit on Jim's shoulder. It was a very strange moment and we took the little bird as a message. If God knows when every sparrow falls, He knew our problem. It gave us courage.

Jim looked at me and I gave him the sad, devastating news. A while later, we went home, each lost in our thoughts and grief. It isn't easy being a wife or hubby at times. We have to be the one to bear bad news and shoulder sadness until our partner gets their bearings and can handle it.

~ ~ ~

A couple of years earlier, Jim had been diagnosed as being bi-polar. It was a difficult time for both of us but we knew that together, with the Lord's help, we could handle anything. It took a while, but we finally had the mental health issues about whipped as long as he stayed on course with his medications. Little did we know the very meds that calmed his mind were attacking his body. The doctors discovered it was the combination of those meds and the chemo drug that fried his kidneys.

Jim had completed his BA in psychology and was working on his

Masters at Texas A&M when the condition asserted itself. He was working for the State of Texas as the Outreach Director in different counties, as an alcoholism and drug abuse counselor, and also took care of the mental health patients.

He was forced to retire and we began to spiral downhill into that black pit of mental illness. It's very hard to make healthy adults do anything, but mental illness presents a special battle.

I had to quit working when he went into kidney failure. He needed full-time care to keep track of his many medications for all the problems he had and to make sure he stuck to his very serious kidney diet. Thank God he had retired from the Navy. His veteran's pension and medical benefits were all that kept us going.

Time slipped away from us. Finally, our doctor at Ft. Sam Houston ordered Hospice for us. We went through three nurses before Almighty God sent me Patsy, our wonderful guardian Angel. Her husband, an Air Force Captain, had died of cancer, so she understood Jim's military mentality. Just before his death, she came out to tell us she was remarrying. Jim would be her last patient.

We made one more trip, to the hospital at Lackland Air Force Base, so the doctors could install a kidney shunt, but the cancer was invading his heart and he was never able to maintain good health long enough to withstand the dialysis.

Much too soon, the day arrived. Twenty-two months after the doctors pronounced the nine- to twelve-month death sentence, Patsy told me, "We don't have much time now. If you need to make peace or have anything you need to say, try to do it."

I knew the day was coming, of course, but still, it was a shock and it took me a couple of days to get my words and emotions together so I could open my heart to him for what might be the last time.

Then she also told me to make my arrangements. That stunned me. I had to do...what? Despite all we'd been through, all the time that had passed, and despite knowing it was coming, I was so unprepared for the reality of the end, for the reality of the decisions that had to be made.

Sometimes, I think the human mind has a kind of anesthetic that kicks in when we're suddenly faced with overwhelming emotion, emotion that would otherwise render us incapable of doing anything except staring into space and crying. It lets us see a little more clearly, and do what we must without collapsing in the pain and anguish that, of course, comes later, when it's over, and we're alone.

Christmas, 1994, our last together, was fast approaching and I asked him what he wanted. He could only stay up for a few minutes at a time, and could barely talk, but he said, "I want a train set."

Perhaps it was something he'd always wanted as a boy and never got. Or maybe a train set was his favorite toy when he was a child. Or it could have just been a whim at the moment. I never asked him why. It didn't matter. A train set he wanted and a train set he got.

We both wanted him home for the holidays and for his final days. As he was being released on Christmas Eve, Jim got an early gift. After 40 years of estrangement, his Oldest Son, Jim Jr., came to the hospital for a reunion. I can't begin to describe that reunion to you except to say that everyone on the ward reacted with a lot of smiles and a lot of tears. Even his doctor, a Colonel, had tears in his eyes.

Once we got him home and in bed, I set up the train set under the tree and in the morning when he woke, I told him Santa Claus had come. I got him up and made him comfortable and he smiled as I sat on the floor and ran the train. It tooted and blew smoke and made train sounds as it rounded the track. He was happy and content and that was all I could hope for.

Later, hospice arrived with our Christmas dinner and small gifts. It was the last of the very sweet days we got to share.

~ ~ ~

The night before Jim died, I went out to our little porch to pray. I always prayed there at night. It was cold and crisp and I had to tell God that Jim was so tired, he couldn't speak. I had to shave, bathe, turn him, and hand feed him. And I asked for mercy for both of us. Then I went to him and told him, "It's OK baby. I will be and I will love you forever. If you need to, go on."

The next morning, January 31, 1995, at 11:11, he turned his head to toward the brilliant sunlight streaming through the window and went on his way to the next life, in Heaven.

On February 3rd, we laid him to rest, with full military honors, at Ft. Sam Houston National Cemetery

After everyone went home and all the hospital equipment had been removed, I sat in my chair by the Christmas tree I just hadn't been able to make myself take down, and picked up that old issue of *Backwoods Home*, started to reread it, and there began the thought. *My job is done here. Now, maybe...just maybe...*

The Journey Begins

The last real conversation Jim and I had was for my birthday in September, 1994. He asked me what I wanted and I told him for him to be well again.

He said, "You know that isn't happening. Go get yourself a birthday present."

He and Patsy had already conspired to give me a little party. She bought a beautiful card for him to sign and a little coconut cake, which was my favorite.

I wanted a subscription to *Backwoods Home* and told him. He told me to go ahead and order it. I had been buying all the new issues as they came out and he would shake his head – he wasn't a country kinda guy.

A few days later, I ordered my very first *Backwoods Home* subscription and the two annual anthologies they had available at the time. I was so anxious to get them, it seemed like they took forever to get to me.

Ohhhhhh, when that brown envelope arrived and I began reading, I was totally amazed at the people who were trying to live the dream, to live off-grid, and be as self-sufficient as possible. That was when I knew, I just knew it was the life I wanted, too. I would totally immerse myself in them. I spent hours reading and dreaming.

As time passed, I found other books I wanted, including some by Claire Wolfe. My first was *101 Things To Do 'til The Revolution*. As I read it, I realized I had found a female hero. She wrote about many things I thought about but had never seen another woman write about – things like her ideas about hiding in plain sight and burying things, which I later used for my money, and having an escape/hiding area away from the house.

She seemed to be a free spirit with more courage than I had ever seen. And she had the courage of her convictions. She truly gave me personal courage and many ideas in my adventures in my new life. I admire her even to this day.

~ ~ ~

I had to sell everything to settle Jim's estate and pay the final expenses, though I saved my 25-gallon propane tank, my twin bed, all my blankets (thank God, because I was going to need them), all my sweats, regular household things and kitchen tools, 2 oil lamps I had for our Texas storms, my hand tools, yard tools, clothes, personal items, camping equipment that would come in real handy, and, of course, my books. I also had power tools – boy would those prove to be useless.

Jim's little dog, Tippy, had begun to grieve. She wouldn't eat and wandered from room to room looking for him, but she finally pulled out of it and would be my companion for another sixteen years.

Death isn't final for the living. There are so many things to shut down, so many forms to fill out. You do all the running, wondering when it will all end. The biggest test was applying for VA widow's benefits. I qualified, but it was almost a year before they finally became active. Returning soldiers and the families of the dead from Desert Storm were given preference. A part of me understood, but another part didn't. It was a small pension, and it would come in time to really help me as I struggled.

~ ~ ~

I had been sharing with my family my dreams of living off-grid. Parts of those dreams were lots of acreage and a small house. One day, my Oldest Son called and said, "Mama, I think I've found the place you were talking about. It's an 80-year-old house on fifty acres."

A friend of his had a few head of cattle on it and wasn't renewing his lease when it came due in May. He said he didn't live there and that I was welcome to the house. The best part – the lease was only five hundred dollars a year! I didn't understand why his friend didn't live in the house and why the lease was so cheap, but I would soon enough.

On March 13th, I left San Antonio with all my belongings in the back of my pickup truck. My first stop was the cemetery, so I could tell Jim good-bye once more. Then I headed down Interstate 10 to Houston to meet up with my Sons so they could take me to Hopewell

Road in Bedias, Texas and to my new adventure or failure or quest or whatever would happen. It would be the greatest adventure and the most loved time of my life.

I was sure I was prepared. After all, I had read all those books I ordered and I had the spirit, the strength, the determination, and the will. Looking back on it now, I can smile. But at the time, I had no idea of the tests that would come, tests that would be builders of intestinal fortitude, that would completely change my mindset and lead me on a physical, mental, and spiritual journey the likes of which I'd never before known.

We left Houston, heading north on Interstate 45, the three boys in Youngest Son's truck with me following them in mine. When we reached Huntsville, we hung a left on Farm Road (Texas 30) west. Of course it had to rain. My stuff was pretty much covered, so I didn't worry, not until we hit the soggy caliche road. I dropped into mud gear and the truck settled into its fun gear, slinging the cream colored mud everywhere, especially up.

We drove until I was sure we'd run out of civilization. Finally, we did, and not long after, we were there – a narrow turn-off, through the gate, into an overgrown yard, and there it was – a little house that had once been white, sitting under the biggest chinaberry tree I had ever seen. I didn't know it then but that massive tree would become a huge pain in my neck, and elsewhere, as it grew even bigger.

Despite the long ride, I was excited and joined them in a round of "We're here. We're here." Then we were all stretching and racing for the bushes – well, my sons were racing. I wasn't too sure yet about embracing that much nature.

As I looked around, I could see a meadow to the left with huge oaks, and as I started to the house, something came over me, a joy I hadn't experienced in a long while, a feeling of "I am home." The feeling was short-lived.

The day was quickly fading and the boys let me know they needed to start home soon. I was a little confused.

"Aren't you boys staying the night?"

"Nope."

"What!?"

I hadn't really realized this was a drop-the-mama-and-run outing. But they did help me unload the truck and then, off they went, after first cleaning the mud off. If you've never experienced it, trust me, there is nothing slimier than wet caliche.

After their truck turned back on to the road, I turned and proceeded to take stock of my new home, which left me with more questions than reassurance.

• There was no bathroom in the house and no outhouse. *Had the folks who lived here years ago trekked out to the bushes every time they had to take care of business?*

• There was no running water and no well I could see. *How did they drink and cook and bathe?*

• There was no power in the house. *What was I thinking moving here?!* (I hadn't been thinking, of course. I'd been dreaming a dream.)

The ole house

In fact there was no nothing, not even cabinets in what I assumed was the kitchen. There was what I thought to be a locked storeroom, but it turned out to be a winter kitchen with a problem – the chinaberry tree. The house had become a leaning post for that tree.

My Oldest had told me it was primitive, but I wasn't worried. I'd read all those books. I'd figure it out in the morning.

Looking closer, I saw the ole house had accumulated years of dust, birds' nests, spider webs, and shed snake skins. Me and Tippy, we decided to sleep in the truck that night, which would be the first of many such nights thanks to skunks and scorpions.

~ ~ ~

With the sunrise the next day came the realization that not only was there no bathroom in the house, or an outhouse, there wasn't even a bucket around to use. Like it or not, I was going to have to learn to embrace nature – or at least the bushes – for a while.

When I took stock of my situation I found I had coffee and sugar but no fire because I had twenty-five gallons of propane but no stove. Not that having a stove would have mattered just then because I had no water.

But I had read all those books!

The nearest store of any kind was at a very small, family-run, two-pump gas station that I discovered was very pricey and very clannish. Across the road was a very small feed/hardware store, which would become a friendly, comic-relief stop-off spot in the future, but that morning, the only feed I wanted was for myself.

When I walked in the door of the gas station's store, I got a 'who is this interloper' look from the woman behind the counter. She may have been suspicious of me, but she took my money for a cup of coffee and a roll, and a gallon jug of water, which I was very happy to find because in those days, bottled water wasn't a stocked item at most small stores. This one carried it because they also sold bait and catered to fisherman.

When I asked where the nearest Walmart was, the owner pointed and said, "Seventeen miles that way."

I sighed, mentally adding the seven miles it took to get where I was meant every time I needed something from there would involve a forty-eight mile round trip, not to mention the gas and wear and tear on the truck.

I went out and shared my roll with ole Tippy, then dug out my hair brush, gave a look in the mirror, and started laughing. I never before went out looking like this – maybe that explained some of the look I got in the store – but this would fast become the norm for me – clean, brushed hair, no make-up, and a new attitude.

I knew exactly what I needed and headed for what turned out to be a very small Walmart seventeen miles away.

~ ~ ~

Say what you will about Walmart, but they do seem to have everything under the sun. I had seen six-gallon, green water kegs at another Walmart, and this one had them, too. I put two of them in my cart along with two half-gallon jugs, a can of bug killer, lamp oil, and (don't laugh) something important I'd forgotten to pack – matches. Over in the pet section, I got Tippy her food. I also bought a small ice chest along with the meat, bread, and sweet rolls which would become a mainstay for me for a few weeks. And a bucket. (Quit laughing!)

On the ride home, I noticed the small-town community hall. There was a fellow mowing the grass, so I stopped and asked if I could get some water. I'm not exactly sure what the look on his face meant when he saw me, but if you remember my appearance, my seriously muddy truck, and where I was...well, I'm pretty sure I gave him back a 'What the hell was I thinking' look. But I got the water.

I was feeling pretty good as I drove home, until I finally realized I missed the turn to the house and had no idea where I was. That's when I kind of panicked. I pulled off to the side of the road, laid my head on the steering wheel and did something I hadn't done for a long time. I sat there and cried. As I sat there raining tears, at some point it really hit me that I'd moved on to a new phase in my life. I was on my own – completely, literally, on my own.

I don't know how long I was parked there feeling sorry for myself, but suddenly a loud horn pulled me back to reality. I looked in the side mirror and saw a big, black Ford dual diesel was parked behind me. A long, tall drink of water ambled up to my window and asked, "Ma'am, you having trouble?" Then he pushed his hat back and added, "I see you're down the road from us."

I took a minute to dry my tears and then told him I missed my turn and got lost, something which isn't hard to do on these old country roads since all oaks look the same – at least they did to me then.

He told me to follow him, and turned to go back to his truck. It was all I could do to get myself together before he climbed into the cab. Then he pulled ahead and I followed him until he honked as he passed my place.

I pulled in and told myself, "Suck it up Annie. You got this. You'll get organized. Slowly, maybe, but it'll all be okay."

I didn't know it at the time, but that was my first glimpse of the man who would become a wonderful neighbor, one who was reclusive and stand-offish, to be sure, but a decent man and a quiet guardian angel.

~ ~ ~

The ole house was built on-site of course-milled planks laid horizontal. And there wasn't a thing between the outside boards and the inside boards but air. Oddly, the interior boards were rougher for some reason. Maybe whoever built it liked the rustic feel of the un-planed boards. Sometime later, I would wish he'd thought to put some insulation between them

It had a wonderful tin roof that would work like a sleeping pill when it rained, but it turned the house into an oven in the summer. The east side appeared to be the new add-on. It was probably only sixty years old instead of eighty years old like the main section, but the framed windows were sagging.

I ventured into the winter kitchen. It was kind of scary as there was only one tiny window, but it did have an outside door. I found the other chimney and discovered my chinaberry tree problem. It had pushed the brick chimney over – well almost over. I could see that when it rained, the water would pour in. At first I thought, "Goodness! What can I do?" but then I realized I wasn't all that crazy about the tiny room anyway.

Since I wasn't going to use the room, I knew I had to close-up that door. The rotted floor would allow all manners of critters in and the last thing I wanted was to have to share the main house with them. I would have to take care of that, and soon.

I opened the south-facing back door and the front door that faced stone-cold north, then began sweeping out years of accumulated dirt and dust and everything else. I killed all manner of critters, including black widow spiders and a few scorpions. The one thing that got me skittish was the snake skins, especially the big one, which turned skittish to paranoid. I kept looking around for the owners of the skins but thankfully, never found them. Or should I say, they never found *me!*

Days go by awfully fast when you're busy and that first full day in my new home was no exception. Besides more cleaning than I had ever-before done in one day, I got my bed set up along with the sleeping bag and blankets I would use on it. I also filled the oil lamps and trimmed the wicks, which was fortunate because I was fast running out of daylight. Finally, I got out my little .25 caliber semi-auto pistol and was prepared for dark. Then, I went outside and looked around as dusk settled over my new homestead.

It was clear the land had been no-better cared for than the house. The grass was high and I was really worried about snakes. But the worry was pushed aside when I looked at the beautiful, 150-year-old oak that stood behind the house. I really loved that tree. It stood and grew through so many Texas summer heats and winter colds, it became, for me, a sort of symbol of what's possible and a reminder that if I persevered, I could overcome anything and flourish. Not that I thought of it that way back then, but I see it clearly now.

Back then, I was wondering how I was going to get bath water, cooking water, dish-washing, and laundry water. Twelve gallons doesn't last very long. I walked around the ole house, looking at the slope of the roof and the solution seemed obvious. Barrels. I needed barrels.

I really needed to make a list, but I would think about it tomorrow. I was totally exhausted, alone, and for the first time in years, I would have to depend solely on me, no one else.

Suddenly I knew fear. Had I lost my mind? Was I chasing a dream or a nightmare? None of it mattered, though. I had no place to go back to. Whatever it was, whatever it took, this was my new home.

Too tired to think more about it, Tippy and I climbed into the sleeping bag. Tomorrow would come soon enough. Then, I began to hear sounds in the attic, gnawing, a lot of gnawing. All I could do was shake my head. One more problem to deal with. I realized I was going to need a list just for problems.

I had to get up in the night to use the new bucket, so I reached for the gun and my Maglite flashlight, got up, and headed to the back porch. As I stepped into the room that would later become my kitchen, there were at seven or eight BIG rats lumbering around the room. They had my sweet rolls.

Tippy and I slept in the truck another night.

~ ~ ~

By the time I woke up the next day, my mind and body had more than enough of sleeping in the truck. Tippy, on the other hand, was curled up on the floor on her blanket, comfortable as can be.

She was a wire-hair terrier mix, her hair a sandy mix of colors. I always thought she had been strained through a sieve or something because her four sisters were snow-white.

She was beginning to love riding in the truck. She knew when we got close to the new house and would stand up and wag her tail. In our years together, she never bit or offered to bite and rarely barked, having been house trained at an early age. And her favorite foods were – I swear – fried chicken and Cheerios.

During our years off-grid, she was shot by a poacher, snake-bit twice, and had a standing appointment with most of the skunks in the area. She spent a lot, and I mean *a lot* of time in the tomato juice bath.

She didn't weigh much more than ten or twelve pounds, but developed the heart of a lion. She was a tall skinny hunter – a rabbit hunter, and frog catcher who knew no fear. And after she figured out how to catch them, rats and moles didn't stand a chance.

I watched her spend hours treeing squirrels. She even tried climbing trees. But with people, she was a gentle ole dog. We had her spayed as a baby, so she had her mind straight.

As I climbed out of the truck, I knew Tippy and I had to get a plan. Maybe she could sleep anywhere, but my body screamed for real rest, I needed real food, and I needed a bath real bad. A spit bath will get ya by, but hey, I don't have to tell you it's nothing compared to a long, hot soak in a tub after a hard day's work.

And I needed to start making those damn lists.

We headed to the feed store/hardware store/kerosene depot where I got the best cup of coffee I'd had in a long while from the ole fellow who worked there, along with, "You're living where? That ain't living. That's existing."

What could I say? I asked about some water/rain barrels.

He said he knew his were too expensive, so he drew me a map to

14

an old used-goods place. He said I could get fifty-five gallon barrels for $5 – my kind of price. And he told me to knock on the door hard because the ole fellow was kind of deaf.

Tippy

As I started to leave, I remembered the rats and asked him what to do to get rid of them. He said his truck would deliver some poison the next day that would knock 'em right out. But he didn't mention how bad the stink would be.

Our southeast Texas spring weather is fickle. I've been at the beach in November and had sleet on Easter. So when I noticed clouds building up, coming in from the north, I knew my mild days had just run out. I decided to go to the used-goods place the next day. Boy, was I in for a surprise.

That night, my water was trying to freeze in the kitchen. Tippy and I had no choice but to sleep in the house. I had on two layers of clothes and Tippy wore her sweater. By morning I was in the truck trying to get warm.

~ ~ ~

The next morning, I had to visit the bucket. As I climbed the back steps I saw something buried in the grass. Kicking at it with my toe, I saw it was a rectangular iron boot-scraper. It looked homemade, about three feet by four feet with bars every inch or so. Sort of like a section of short, iron fence. I suppose with all the mud the rain brought, having a boot-scraper would have been nice, but I had other, more urgent needs. The boot-scraper would soon become the top of my cook-stove.

It's a funny thing. When you live with all the comforts of modern life, an old boot-scraper half-buried the tall grass is a curiosity, at best. More likely, it's a piece of junk that ends up in the trash pile. But I wasn't in the city anymore. My mind was starting to rise out of the dark and the grieving into survival mode.

I had enough deadfall to keep a wood stove going for a long time. What I needed, now were some concrete blocks.

I washed up in the coldest water that had ever touched my face. If I'd been dead tired, that water would have woken me right up. Then I pulled on a cap to hide my tousled hair and headed to the junk store – I mean, the used-goods store.

It felt like I drove forever to get there, but as soon as I came up on the place, I spotted my life-saver – an old sheet metal wood-burning stove sitting in the yard. I can't tell you how happy I was to see my future source of heat right there, like it was waiting for me. I also saw an old enamel bath-tub and my brain started clicking again. How much money did I have?

The ole fellow came out, all bundled up against the cold, and we introduced ourselves. I asked him how much he wanted for the wood-burner and told him I also needed water barrels. After a little back and forth, I got the wood burner for $18, two water barrels for $5 each, plus he gave me the tub for free, said it wouldn't hold water because the drain had been messed up when the people took it out.

Thank goodness I always carried rope behind my seat. I tied down my treasures and headed to the feed store for some stove pipe. I had a pretty good idea of what I needed to do and bought what I figured I needed. Of course I was wrong, as I'd find out soon enough.

I headed home and when I pulled into the yard, there sat my Middle Son. I couldn't help but smile at his timing. Boy, did I have a job or two for him

He and I assessed the situation. Then he said we should go out to the dump pile at the back of the property. I had no idea it was there. I suppose it would have been a good idea to walk the land when I arrived, but I had more urgent concerns and never even thought of it. When we got there, we found a treasure trove of goodies, including concrete blocks, a piece of sheet of metal to put under the wood-burning stove, and an old rocking chair.

After we hauled it all back, getting heat into the house became the first order of business. I was cold and hungry, but the sun was out, which helped take my mind off how I was feeling.

We set the wood stove on the sheet metal and blocks, then looked at how to vent it outside. There was really only one good choice. The stove pipe would have to go through the old cracked window. Before I could even consider how to do it, he told me he had just the thing, an old hubcap he found in the dump pile.

Middle Son is a painter by trade and he had his ladder and tools. If only he'd arrived earlier in the morning, before I left, we probably wouldn't have had to make another trip to get the right elbows.

That night, sitting by that ole wood-burner by lamp light, I felt peace for the first time in a long while, even though the wind whistled through the ole house. Another problem for the list.

He stayed overnight and slept in his truck.

~ ~ ~

The next morning we took both trucks to the back of the fifty [acre lot] and loaded them up with deadfall. While we were there, we saw the cattle in a meadow. One mama had given birth to a tiny, snow white bull calf with a black line down his back. We called him zipper. Calves always seem to be born when it's cold.

The twelve head of cattle all came wandering up to the trucks, no doubt looking for a treat. The bull rubbed himself on my tail-gate, rocking the truck, but he seemed friendly enough. I would find out how friendly one night, in the dark.

The owner of the cattle was the friend my Oldest Son knew, the person who told him about this new place I was living at. He was a lineman and always hayed and fed field chunks – compact feed cubes – to the cattle in the winter.

After a while, we took a break and walked down a trail that led to a beautiful pond. I had wondered how the cattle were watered. The pond seemed full of activity and since I was a fisherman – or fisherwoman – from way back, I knew what I would be soon be eating. And did. All through the years I lived there I enjoyed the small bass and frying-pan-sized perch I caught.

We started back to the ole house. Crossing the trail was a doe with two fawns. She was crippled in her right hind leg. I was surprised she didn't run. We just sat there watching them as she watched us. I suspected she had been eating with the cattle and thought we might have food too. I saw her often, through the years. She had more fawns, in a little shaded, covered area, kinda like a birthing area.

It took us awhile to unload and stack the firewood. Then we set up my cooking area – the boot scrapper over 3 concrete blocks – and got a fire going before I took out my camping coffee pot and had the first of many cups of coffee brewed in that old, speckled pot. I still have her today.

I learned about keeping my wood dry that week. It rained and rained and stayed cold. But that was alright. I had lots of cleaning to do and two lists to make – a problems list and a needs list.

As we heated some spam over the fire in my cast iron skillet, I had a feeling, a realization. My great adventure was underway. Not long after, my son said, "Mama come back into town with me. It's not safe out here. We're worried about you."

I understood their concern and appreciated they wanted to look out for me, but I had to heal and to find my way my own way.

~ ~ ~

I had nowhere to put my pots and pans, so they stayed in a box. I kept my clothes in a duffle bag because I had no closet to hang my things. I wondered what the people who lived there before me had done for closets.

Before he left, my son put the rat bait in the attic. The constant chewing began to stop and thank goodness. It was driving me nuts! And the nasty things had eaten my sweet rolls and tried my canned spam – yuck.

Sitting in the cold ole house, it began to dawn on me that, for the first time, I didn't have anyone to take care of. The place was so empty, so quiet. There was almost no traffic noise. I would hear maybe three or four cars or trucks and the school bus twice a day.

I began to shake, though I don't know if it was from fear, relief, or sheer aloneness. Lots of folks don't like being alone, don't understand being alone. So many of us are with family or co-workers all day long, we always have people all around us. But suddenly, here I was, seven miles from the nearest store that was little more than a gasoline pit stop, twenty-four miles from the nearest "civilization," Madisonville, and thirty miles from Huntsville. I think I really began to realize just how much I'd bitten off and how much I would have to chew and swallow to realize my dream of off-grid self-reliance. So I bundled up to go outside, walk around, and get some fresh air to maybe clear my head. I had to decide if this was what I wanted or needed to do and where I wanted to live.

I walked over to the big oak behind the house. In the tall grass and weeds, I saw a pile of junk and wondered what in the world made someone pile old tires and bed-springs under the tree when there was a perfectly good dumping ground at the back of the property.

Deciding to get busy to get rid of this terrible feeling, I moved the truck around. As I loaded the trash, I saw a round mound of rocks and cement. It was a hole in the ground! As I cleared more stuff away for a closer look, oh man! I was tickled to death and started jumping up and down. Now I knew how the folks got their water – an in-ground cistern.

A cistern!

But I didn't have a bucket. Well, I did, but it was already doing potty duty.

I got the flashlight out of my truck, shined the beam in for a look and wow! She was full of water. Then it dawned on me that the cattle would smell the water, come for a drink, and fall in. That's why it had been covered up. So I drug the bed springs and tires off the truck and covered the cistern up again. But I could mark water off my problems list. And the cows would be gone in a few weeks.

I had water. Now to make it work for me.

I made my decision. I would stay and make a life for myself.

~ ~ ~

I felt like it was never going to warm up. I kept the ole wood burner fired up and sat real close.

19

That night, as I looked at my lists, I saw I needed some #3 washtubs and remembered seeing them at the feed store.

A plan had formed in my head and I decided I'd go get a couple. I would set up my tubs for dish washing near the cistern because it would be a whole lot easier baling water into them if they were close to the cistern. Oh yeah...I needed a bucket. I added that too my list, then wondered if I should buy two buckets. Buckets are handy things to have but I was short on money so I only bought the one.

When I went to bed that night and lay there in the dark, it seemed like everything in the house moved, cracked, squealed, and wiggled. Sleep was a while coming.

The next morning, I got up and fired up my boot-scraper-on-concrete-blocks stove, made coffee, and thought to myself, *I can't handle these grounds anymore.* I'd been making coffee by boiling the grounds in the water, and, of course, some grounds always ended up in my cup when I poured. I dug through my utensils and found my little strainer. No more coffee grounds. It was a small thing, sure, but I already had to fight various critters for sole possession of the house and darn well didn't want to have to fight my coffee to enjoy it.

After I drove to the store to get my tubs and bucket, I went down to the dump, which was really an old dry creek bed, and dug though it until I uncovered some more blocks. I would later learn the blocks were to be part of a smoke house that never got built. Why the blocks, being such useful things and in good shape, ended up in the dump, I never learned. The same with a lot of the stuff I found there. I guess it's true that one person's trash is another's treasure.

I set my tubs up on the blocks and lit fires under them to heat the water. Of course, the wind was coming in from the south and blew the smoke straight through the house. Geezzzz...I felt like a dummy. But I learned another lesson. So in the winter, the fire was built on the south side of the oak and in the summer, the north side of the oak.

I uncovered the cistern and started baling water. A note here to those of you who may, in the future, have a similar cistern – remember to tie off the bucket! I didn't, and it would be a few years, during a terrible drought, before I would find the bucket again at the bottom of an almost dry cistern.

Right about this time, the cows came up to call on me, maybe to get a look at the idiot who dropped her bucket in the cistern. But I was in no mood to play with cattle so I quickly put out the fires, covered the cistern, and went back inside.

For many years, I would think about those early days, all the mistakes I made and all I learned by making them. It seemed like my mind did not want to function like I wanted it too. I came to realize it was mostly just the grief of losing Jim mixed with the sudden change in comfort levels that made me absent-minded. But I felt lucky to even be feeding myself and I wasn't going to worry too much about forgetfulness and such. Time would take care of that.

A few days later, as I was warming myself in the house, I realized the cows were coming to the front of the property and wondered why. I finally realized why, though, when I heard a truck at the gate. The fellow had come to feed them and see his new calf. How they knew he'd be coming is a mystery I never solved, but I think they could hear the truck quite a-ways off.

I told him I named the calf Zipper and he asked me when it was born, then recorded it on a pad he brought. A while later, his lady friend came, too. She knocked on the door and asked if I wanted lunch. I sure did. I wasn't about to turn down free food.

We sat on the tailgate of his truck and had bologna sandwiches with chips and drinks. It tasted like a steak dinner after the spam I'd been eating.

We talked and the fellow asked me, "Anne what are you doing out here by yourself?"

All I could say was, "I am going to live here."

He was shaking his head when she offered me a job at Krogers. Turns out she was some kind of big wig in the company. I'd worked in retail before and the very thought of having to deal with people made me shake. I moved from the city to get away from crowds of people. But I didn't know how to tell her that, so I just thanked her and said I'd think about it.

He told me a little about the area. He said that Hopewell Road was ten miles long and if I took a right at the end of it, it was a shorter way to get to Huntsville. To this day, I don't believe it. You can drive until you run out of road out there – really.

He told me about the two black churches on Hopewell Road. The congregation had split decades ago and they built another church across the road. Despite their differences, they all liked the pastor, who went to each church every other Sunday. He also told me about Mustang Cemetery, a really beautiful and peaceful place that was filled with magnificent oak trees.

When the time came for them to leave, he drove to the back and the cows followed, all except the bull. He liked my truck and would stand right next to it. I sometimes wondered if he thought it was a big cow and was waiting for it to send him the signal it was ready for him.

~ ~ ~

MONEY:

Looking back over the days shortly after Jim died, I wondered if I'd ever get it all straightened out.

Jim was a conscientious man. In the time before he became bedridden, he always had a life-insurance policy. When the nurse told me to make my arrangements (I came to hate that term), I called our agent, who told me Jim had called and cancelled the policy because he couldn't afford it. I was dumbfounded. But that was his mental illness talking. This was just another of the many problems it caused.

One time, he loaned money to a friend to get a book published. It was a scam. He would buy pounds of plums which would go bad before he ate them. He often did strange things. His medication only stabilized him in the most minor way.

His cancelling the life insurance caused me great grief. I had to sell the small mobile home we had. Before Jim became bed-ridden, a friend and I had re-floored it and I painted and built small cabinets, but still, it didn't bring much. Jim was cremated as to his wishes, which was a blessing as it was not as expensive as a full burial would have been.

Jim was Catholic and a nun from the church came to see me shortly after he died. She talked with me awhile and when she got ready to leave she handed me money. I was really shocked. She said they kept a small collection in the ladies organization and gave it to folks in need. Boy, was I in need. I had used everything in my checking account to pay for his burial, the rent on our trailer lot, and the utilities. I had about $17.00 to my name that day and was racing to figure out a way to take care of everything. She gave me $281.00 and

I would live on that until I got the mobile home sold.

The day before the folks came to pay me for the home, I had a huge yard sale. What I couldn't sell, I gave to the different folks. I had dozens of potted plants that were my little hobby. I gave them away, too. But I saved my books, my precious books.

His illness would cause me a long court battle for settling his estate because he had an ongoing lawsuit, worth a small sum.

My life in the next 8 years would require hundreds of phone calls and appearances before a probate judge in San Antonio before I was finally appointed administrator of his estate. Why did it take so long? Since Jim had died without a will, the court had to appoint someone to carry out the court's instructions. In Texas, dying without a will is like giving the state a free hand with your possessions. The court decides who gets what and the involved lawsuit really muddied the waters. After the first six years, the lawsuit was settled, but it still took the court another 2 years to settle the estate, which was ludicrous, as we had nothing but what might come from the lawsuit.

The probate lawyer was a doll, absorbing the cost until the final days of the lawsuit and settlement of the estate. His paralegal shed as many tears as I did.

It would have been easier in those first years if I had a phone, but cell phones were in their infancy and expensive then, and there was no phone line running by my house. When I finally got a cell phone some years later, I would have to stand on a ladder in a pasture to get a signal. I even did it in the dark to keep in touch with everyone.

~ ~ ~

I knew sooner or later I would lose the truck, even though I only owed about nine payments. I needed a job, but I had to get my living arrangements settled. It's one thing to live rough for a short time, and things were rough when it came to comfort, that's for sure. But it's another thing for it to go on and on and on just existing, as the guy from the hardware store said that day. I really was just existing, but I was determined to start living again.

I made the decision to live out here because it was where I knew, in my heart, I always wanted to be. It was where I belonged. So I knew I would survive and carve out a life. Sometimes dreams are stronger than what life throws at us. At least mine were back then. I had absolutely no doubt that I would live my dream. I was in my early fifties, I was not a wallflower – not by a long shot – and I was in good physical health, although, despite my determination, there were times I doubted my sanity. Even with all the problems the move brought me in the beginning, somehow I knew it would be okay.

As difficult as many things were, there were also great pleasures, even from the start. I loved the smells in the morning – the pines, the great oaks, the clean air. But I had to get used to the quietness. It was nerve racking for a while and I would sometimes shake with fear. The feeling of being alone was scary, especially for a former city girl. But those episodes became fewer as I threw myself into rebuilding my life and rebuilt my confidence and self-esteem the right way, with accomplishments big and small, and lessons learned.

Speaking of which, I got another bucket and yes, I tied it off. (Stop laughing!)

I got my two #3 tubs set up and full of water, started it to heating, and then drug the old tub to the back porch and stopped up the drain with Tippy's tennis ball. When the water was hot enough, I transferred it to the tub and had me a bath, right out in the open. It sure was cold as I undressed, but once I was in the tub, well...there's nothing like hot water and a good soak to make you forget your troubles. If anyone was sneaking around in the woods and saw me nekkid, oh well. That bath felt much too good for me to care.

I'd been used to relatively hard water, but the cistern water was so soft, I had to cut back on the amount of soap. It left my hair so glossy and my skin feeling wonderful.

Those hot tub baths became my therapy sessions. I did eventually get a roll of heavy plastic and turned the back-porch into a sauna. It helped with the cold by blocking the wind and there'd be no more free shows for anyone lurking out in the woods!

As time passed, I would use a lot of that plastic and my faithful old T-50 staple gun, which was the best way to hang it because the wood walls were so hard that if you tried to drive a nail, sparks flew.

I eventually bought a solar shower from Wally World (Walmart) for my hair and set it up out there. It would warm the water just enough to make the shower comfortable. I used it so much I went through two of them in the years I was there.

I also had my towels and soap and general girl stuff out there, including an old mirror that was hanging on the wall when I arrived. Clearly, someone else had done the same thing, using the back-porch as a bathroom. And since bathrooms are for more than just bathing...well, let's be honest. My old five-gallon bucket potty left much to be desired, which I quickly figured out in the middle of one of those cold nights. What I needed was an outhouse. Installing one would become a hilarious adventure.

~ ~ ~

No electricity meant no television. I didn't miss it, except perhaps for the noise. I did miss a having a blow dryer for my hair – a lot – but I learned to towel dry and go stand in the wind and comb it dry.

To replace the TV noise, I had a boom box. That's a big, powerful stereo radio for you young'uns who only know how to listen to music on your iWhatevers. The boom box needed batteries so I became a regular at the Dollar Store battery case. I always bought ahead and kept a good supply of them on hand.

I discovered fire-starter cubes and fire sticks and later I would learn to put pine cones in a coffee can with a little kerosene on them and use them to get the wood burner going in the morning.

My reading had taught me about the danger of fires from creosote buildup in my stove pipes from burning softwoods, so I changed out my interior pipes every winter, just to be safe. I knew if the ole house ever caught on fire that it would burn for days. That old-time cured wood was tough for me to deal with and I figured it would give flames a hard time, too. But I didn't want to ever find out, for sure.

I set the old rocking chair we found on the front porch. It had a deerskin back and as the years passed, it shed the hair and became slick. I used one of the old milk crates we found at the dump site for my side table.

In the evenings, I sat on the porch reading; sometimes listening to the radio, sometimes to nature, and planning the things I needed to do and wanted to do. I'd often make one of the lists that, through the years, would become a part of my life. And I learned not to leave them at home.

~ ~ ~

I've always said *Trouble Rides a Fast Horse*. It often showed up at my door. Sometimes, though, his sibling, *Opportunity*, stopped by.

My first job came unexpectedly. I was sitting on the porch in the sun one morning when a BMW stopped in front of my gate and a woman got out. She was well dressed and visibly upset.

She was looking for someone to help her clean a house, a really beautiful cottage with a clear artesian well. It was fed by a pure, underground stream. I loved that water, and I'm sure so did the many other folks who benefited from it. She and hubby were divorcing and the house was to be put up for sale. She said she would pay well to help her.

I probably should have realized that when she said "help," it would mean "do it all." She was so distraught over the divorce she was basically useless, but I dove right in. I told her I would do the yard first as it was the biggest problem with a lot of old construction leftovers scattered around; leftovers like pieces of plywood and pipe. I knew immediately what I could use that "trash" for.

I made 4 trips to my dump site, trying to sort as I went, but I had to hurry. I worked all day. When I was done with the trash, I mowed the lawn. And she wasn't really useless. She did go to the tiny, four-table cafe and got us burgers. Wow! A gourmet meal again, complete with a chocolate malted. Outstanding!!

Once the lawn was done, she told me that was enough for the day and that she would be back tomorrow. I was earning some much-needed money and would even gain a few pieces of furniture in the deal.

Life was good.

~ ~ ~

It was almost 11 o'clock when she showed up the next morning with a teenage boy in tow. He turned out to be her son.

I drove more loads to the dump, but these were all for the burn pile section. I got all the good, usable stuff yesterday.

Once that was done, we cleaned the house. Mostly, it was just dusty. And we, with the help of her son, moved the furniture to the living room, which had beautiful French doors. The movers were coming the next day.

It's a good thing I had physical strength because there was a lot of furniture.

There was a very old enamel table in the kitchen. White with a green border. It was love at first sight. As we packed dishes, she asked me if it would hurt my feelings if she gave me that table and a chest of drawers. Was she kidding? No, I told her, it wouldn't hurt my feelings. My insides were jumping with joy.

I made one more trip to the dump and was about beat. When I returned, she had her son help me load my prizes. I was now the proud owner of a real enamel-topped table and a huge chest of drawers. Bingo! Now, my clothes could come out of the bags. I was slowly moving away from existing toward human living again.

When my stuff was all loaded and tied down, she paid me. I was taken aback by how much. Then she asked if I would come down to check on the house for her, adding that she would pay me. She handed me a business card, then looked at me and asked what had happened. Why was I living out here alone and in these conditions?

I kinda choked up and all I could answer was, "Life. Life happened."

Later on I thought about it. She was well-dressed, had lots of money, a fine car, a home, a vacation home, and was miserable. She was feeling sorry for me and I felt so sorry for her. I thought I had the better deal.

As tired as I was, I had to unload my beautiful old table. I set her up in my someday-kitchen, stood back, and admired it. For years, I would sit there in the winter and look out at the meadow, where the deer fed so peacefully. In spring, I'd watch wild flowers bloom. And always, I'd be reading my *Backwoods Home Magazine* and my *Countryside* magazines. I especially liked reading Claire Wolfe, whom I admired. I'd study *Country Self-Sufficiency* by Pete Mickelson, and all my anthologies from *Backwoods Home*. And sometimes, on stormy nights, when I felt overwhelmed, when I'd worry, I'd cry. Grief is a dark master, but I slowly began to function again. It wasn't happening right away, but it was happening.

~ ~ ~

The next day, I dragged the chest of drawers in, with no teenage boy to help. It felt good to put things away, to feel more settled in. I could set my lamps up. I'd been living in fear of turning one over.

True to my word, I would go check on Lady's house. I had a gate key. It was a sad business, though, and I thought this might not be a good job for me. But I needed the money and couldn't be choosy.

I pulled out of the yard one day just in time to meet The Postman. That began a long friendship – not a romantic one – but of two old fogeys against the young'uns.

He drove a long route – 160 miles a day – and had lived out there for 30 years after retiring from the Houston Fire Department.

I had rented a post office box in the tiny town, but it hadn't occurred to me until then to wonder what my address was, so I asked him and he said he'd check and stop by the next day. When he came by the next day, he asked me if I would clean for him once a week.

"Of course," I said.

There's a certain kind of trust you can feel in some people. You just know they're the good, decent kind. He was one of those.

That following week I followed him to his house so I would know where he lived. And wow, he had a huge firewood business going. I was totally amazed.

He explained to me, "You remember seeing those bundles of wood at Walmart for sale? That's what we do here."

I didn't know it then, but I would one day go to work there doing dangerous, dirty, grueling work that would be a life-saver for me.

For now, though, I began cleaning once a week for him. And he, knowing I had no electricity, told me, "If you need to keep meat or some things cold, I have an extra freezer on the back porch. I'll put a lock on it. It'll be yours."

I asked him, "How much?"

He said, "How about five dollars?"

It sounded like an absolute bargain to me, but he never did let me pay him. He'd always say, "Oh it's okay, hun. Catch me later."

When I moved out there in March, I remembered seeing a funeral pass by on the way to Mustang cemetery. I learned it was his wife. She had died suddenly.

It was strange how the fear and loneliness started to creep away. I was still alone, but now I had a connection to another human, six miles down the road.

It would be warming up soon – sure it would – after a bone-chilling nor'easter blew through.

And I had the scare of my life.

~ ~ ~

Overnight, it turned very cold. The frigid wind was whipping through the house. I banked the wood stove and put the sleeping bag on the bed, again. Between that and the blankets, Tippy and I would stay warm.

I had to figure out how to close up the old kitchen door and the hole in the roof, where most of the wind got in. I'd already stapled a piece of plastic over that hole, but it didn't help much. It was more of a fake comfort.

I ate my sweet rolls and fed Tippy, then put her sweater on her and under the covers she went. I tried to read, but my mind drifted. I was getting protein hungry. I needed to go to town and shop and I had to think about cooking outside. But I was tired. I crawled into the sleeping bag listening to a lone rat chewing in the attic. That was okay, though. One was easy to take care of. Soon, I dozed off for what I hoped would be a good night's rest.

Right.

Sometime during the night, I was awakened by a loud racket and shot up out of the bed. Grabbing my flashlight and gun, I headed into my soon-to-be kitchen. The door of the ole house didn't have anything as modern as locks. It had brackets where you could put a 2x6 brace across the door to prevent it from being opened.

I eased the brace off. I'm not one to worry about boogie men and I had to know what was out there.

I had the light under my arm and the pistol in my hand. As I yanked the door open, I pointed the light at what I thought was a human trying to break in, but it turned out to be my new friend, the bull, trying to get on the porch to get warm. I scared him so bad, he tried to wheel around to get off the porch. Now, a twelve hundred pound bull don't wheel gently. He tore up my plastic sauna, turned the tub over, and scared all the cows so that they took off, knocking over my #3 tubs and kicking apart my outdoor stove. Then, there were all the cow patties. Apparently when cows get scared, they let go. Or maybe they were standing there a long time. Either way, geez! Still, I wouldn't see all the damage until morning.

A bull trying to get warm ain't like a cuddly kitten. He's big, and strong, and ugly. I slammed the door shut, put the brace back, then looked at the silly .25 caliber pistol, started laughing, and soon was shaking from both fear and relief at the thought of a bull wanting to get in the house. The laughing turned into a bad case of the giggles as I remembered the bull on the porch. I realized that old wood would have held him. And I figured Big Ugly liked me. At least I knew he liked my truck because that's where he was the next morning, cozying up to my truck. Thankfully, when they fled, the cows had gone back to the back pasture and stayed there.

It wouldn't be long, though, before they would be gone.

~ ~ ~

Of course it rained.

When I got up that morning and looked outside, I was amazed at the destruction. Everything was turned over. There was cow poop all over and plastic blowing in the wind. My soap, shampoo, towels and everything else was all over the place. Helped by the wind, the #3 tubs had rolled out into the meadow and all the bottles had been stepped on and squished.

But the bucket was still hanging out at the oak. See, every cloud really does have a silver lining. (Stop laughing.)

I looked around at the ruin and shook my head. I thought, *no I will clean this up later*. I already had a plan for the day. That kind of thinking was to become the most important thing in my struggle for survival. Make a plan and try to stay on course.

I had shopping to do and things to buy but it was so cold, I decided to take ole Tippy with me. I didn't feel comfortable leaving her alone in the house. It was well that I did.

When I came back much later that day, I found the gate standing open, which was a no-no because the cows could have wandered out. Then I discovered someone had kicked in the door and ransacked the house. Later on, I would find out it didn't end there.

~ ~ ~

I could hear the mama cow out in the field bawling and bawling, even into the night. But I was too busy trying to see evidence I could collect. All my canned meat was gone. The drawers were all pulled out of the chest and all my clothes dumped on the floor. Thank goodness I'd brought the pistol with me that morning.

It gets dark about 6 PM in the winter and I still had to bring in my groceries. But I needed to run and call the sheriff, and I didn't even know my address. I headed back out to the gas station. Thank God someone was listening to me on the pay-phone and told me the name of the road I lived on.

An old Deputy Sheriff showed up. He was nearing retirement and would later become the county Constable. Many Texas counties have them to serve warrants and such. The way he looked at the tire tracks, I could tell he was a real tracker and that he had a clue. He knew every old truck and every good ol' boy in the county.

While he was looking around, I had to put my groceries on top of the chest of drawers. I had grabbed a sack of ice for the little cooler, where I put my butter, half-gallon of milk, and a package of chicken.

When he was finished, he told me to lock up, then turned and looked me dead in the eyes and said, "Defend yourself."

I got the message and set the brace in the door after he was gone.

I was glad I hadn't picked up the tubs that morning. I figured they would have stolen them also.

I ate a can of Vienna sausage and some sweet rolls, then decided I was too tired to go on and went to bed. As I lay there I kept hearing the cows calling. I knew they were calling for another member of the herd and hated the feeling I had. Still, I bundled up and dozed off, listening to the wind and the rain and cows mooing.

~ ~ ~

I didn't even start my coffee when I woke up. I'd have to reset my stove, since those who broke in had knocked it off the blocks and busted one of them. I jumped in the truck to go to the back of the lot. My God the sight was horrifying.

The little white calf was on the ground, bloodied. He'd been shot and his hind quarters were gone. I turned, gagging and crying. The

31

mama cow didn't help. She still mooed for the calf to nurse.

I thought, *dear Lord who was so cruel.*

I knew I had to get the Sheriff back. I drove to the house and when I got there, he was sitting at the locked gate. I opened it and told him he needed to go to the back, that they had killed a calf. He swore like a good country boy and headed out to the herd.

When he returned, I gave him the number of the fellow who owned the calf and he said he'd take care of it. He also said this was a signature and that he had an idea who had done this.

I was still bawling, madder than hell, and wanted my own vengeance. I hoped they came back.

I didn't understand why they did it. Zipper wasn't but a few weeks old. He was still skinny and growing, no meat really. I finally put it down to pure cruelty. The sight of that poor calf remained with me for a long time.

The cows' owner showed up after work the next day. He didn't speak, which I didn't understand for years, until I had lived among the ranchers. Each death and/or the theft of a cow is a sad thing to them. It was the same as working all week and someone stealing your pay-check, but a lot more up-close and personal. Cattle are a ranchers living.

Zipper's owner buried him. The mother mooed for another day and then hushed. Even Big Ugly, the bull, seemed subdued.

I decided this silly little pistol wasn't going to cut it. I needed a big bang machine to deal with people who would do things like that. My sister-in-law had given me the pistol while we were in San Antonio. It was an easy carry gun but really inadequate for my situation, isolated and alone.

The day before, I had gotten a few other things in town on my grocery run. I had spotted a Stihl chainsaw shop. I needed an axe, a good one. There, I found my perfect workmate. It had a beautiful oak handle. I asked for a file to keep her sharp and I got instructions on how to sharpen her. In the years to come, that axe would be my most modern equipment. She and I split many a cord of wood together.

I needed to do laundry and remembered seeing a pawn shop when I left the chainsaw shop. Gas and wear and tear on the truck cost money, so I always tried to make every trip count and get as much done as possible.

I loaded up the dirty clothes and Tippy and I went off to town. Tonight, I would have clean clothes and would also sleep better. I would have a weapon to back up my mouth.

When I walked into the pawn shop, I went right to the wall of rifles and shotguns and spotted one with a beautiful dark oak stock.

It was a .20 gauge Mossburg. The fellow behind the counter told me it didn't have the kick of a lot of shotguns and he was right. She didn't, which I discovered as I learned how to shoot and very quickly reload.

Now come steal my stuff and kill another calf you damn hateful humans. Come on.

I never again left the house without both guns. I still have the Mossburg. And I still have the same attitude.

~ ~ ~

You may have gathered I'm not a big fan of being cold, so you'll understand why I got up the next morning and was happy to find the sun had popped out and was warming things up. I had a major clean-up to get to and was hoping Big Ugly and his girls would stay in the back.

My first task was to fetch the #3 tubs and set them back up. Then I baled water from the cistern to fill them. Through the years I would bail thousands of buckets of water and filling my tubs, then starting the fires to warm the water, became a ritual I did without thinking.

My best guess was that the cistern was about twenty-five to thirty feet deep and about four feet wide. It appeared to have a shale-like liner, maybe a high-calcium mix of concrete and small rocks. I was amazed how it stood strong through the years, serving those who lived here, and then waiting years for me to arrive and discover it again.

I knew I had a long day of cleaning and repairing and redoing my sauna ahead of me, so I made my coffee as the tubs of water heated, enjoying the smell of the oak-wood smoke. I hadn't been able to find the cover to the coffee pot, and when it was done, I noticed it had picked up a bit of flavor from the smoke.

Cooking outdoors quickly became just a thing I did and didn't even think about, though once I went to work at the wood yard, I started craving a stove in the house.

My next task was to get the shovel and clean up the...cow-evidence. I put it a pile to use as garden fertilizer. Then I started on the repairs.

Keeping busy was taken care of for me. Living in this place never left time to be bored.

Tomorrow was my day to clean The Postman/friend/business owner's house. There I would meet some strange folks.

When I first arrived in the area, I found an isolationist mentality in the folks who lived here. And as I got more comfortable with remote living, I found myself adopting that same mindset.

When you're isolated, you become more aware, more thoughtful, and more inventive. You're on your own, responsible for yourself and everything needed to keep going, and you either quickly figure that out and learn to be more self-sufficient, or you won't survive.

I was determined to survive.

Though there were times when I felt the loneliness, I loved being alone, responsible only to and for myself. I became stronger, both mentally and physically, as my mind freed itself and my body responded to the strength training, also known as hard work.

Things became so much clearer and I fell in love with this life I chose and lived on my terms – well, as far as nature would let me.

I caught myself looking across the meadow toward the house, watching the sun stream through the beautiful oaks, with the smell of the pines filling each breath, and smiled. And I swear to this day, the ole house smiled back.

~ ~ ~

I said in the beginning that this is not fiction. But I want to explain why I gave the people that came into my life adjective type names instead of using their real names.

For one thing, I've lost touch with many of them, and it would be difficult or impossible to get their permission to name them. Also, some of the things that happened along the way...well, some folks might not be comfortable with having their real names attached, like

Lady, who went through a painful divorce. I've always valued my own privacy and feel it is only right to respect theirs.

I also wanted to talk about how amazed I was at the different personalities I encountered and at all the levels of knowledge. Just like in an on-grid city, folks living off-grid came in all types. Most were friendly, but many were difficult. Heck, even some friendly folks could be difficult under the right circumstances.

Many of them resented the intrusion of new folks. I don't think it was mistrust as much as it was that the lives they led kept them so busy, they really didn't have time to educate new folks into the way of The Road. That's what Hopewell Road was called by those who lived along and off her – simply The Road.

The Road was ten miles long, with many side roads into the woods. As time passed, I learned the sound of people's cars and trucks and at night, in the dark, I would be able to say to myself, there goes so-in-so. And when their kids learned to drive, I knew when it was the kids by the way they tested the limits of the vehicle. And like most folks along The Road, I would immediately know when a stranger's vehicle passed and my mind went on alert.

From my porch, I watched many funeral processions pass on their way to Mustang cemetery. It was a unique place; beautiful, quiet, and very dignified.

There were two wooden bridges on The Road spanning what were normally dry creek beds. When we had ten- to twelve-inch rains, both would wash out. Of course the new idiots just had to try to make it across anyway and ended up stuck there, bobbing up and down. I can't tell you how many cars had to be pulled out of the creeks.

The last seven miles of The Road was a caliche/rock mixture, but my part was plain caliche – a miserable, dirt and a mud-lover's dream. Mud would ball up under fender wells and stop you in your tracks. And wet, it was a driving task-master. The rule was to stay in the ruts and not be a hot-dogger and try to make new ones because it would make driving more difficult for those coming later. Sometimes, new folks would first meet a neighbor when one of the old-timers would show up at their door and advise them of that fact!

~ ~ ~

As I tried to make my broken-down house into a home, I often

35

wandered around the fifty acres. On one of these early walks, I discovered a pond on the other side of the meadow. It was a hog wallow and that's when I learned about the wild hog problem. I didn't realize how dangerous it was to walk in on a herd of them and disturb an old boar. They are very dangerous when they feel the herd is threatened.

Ranchers hated them. They rooted up grassland and the dumb cows would stumble and break legs. And, of course, where I lived, the cows were kings and queens of the pastures with a royal right to graze it.

Sound carried farther in the winter, and I would hear the hog hunters when it was cold. They hunted with dogs and many of the dogs lost the fight. An old tusker could rip a dog open in one swipe. The trick was to breed dogs that were big and strong. They were taught to grab the ears and for some reason that would bring the hogs down.

I would one day have a unique experience with a litter of orphaned piglets and one special little girl pig that came to think she was a dog. She was hilarious. I had a built-in entertainment center with her.

As I walked back to the house, two brothers – one about fifteen, the other twelve – rode by on their horses. Of course they stopped to chat. They were kind of sad boys, but as time went by, the older one would become a friend. Their folks were the hell-raisers on The Road and one day, he asked if he could visit. I was a little hesitant, but as the mother of three boys, I could hear it in his voice. He needed to talk. Over the years, he would visit often. I watched him grow up and at times, my heart broke for him.

You may escape the city, but the problems seem to be the same, just isolated more.

~ ~ ~

When spring finally came, it was warm enough to take down the plastic on the interior kitchen door and try to put something over it to close it solid.

It seemed like nothing in the house was square or plumb, including the walls and floor of this room. You almost had to duck down to walk through the door.

I knew there was a piece of plywood in the dump, so I took the truck back and got it. When I arrived back with it, I immediately saw

36

some problems. Always, there had to be problems. First, my salvaged piece of plywood was too tall. I knew my hand saw wouldn't cut through it and I didn't have electricity for my Skill saw. What to do?

At the old back porch, there was about a two-foot step down. The lights came on. If I laid the plywood just right I could jump off on it and break it. Brilliant! And it worked. The break wasn't clean, but it was workable. About six weeks later, as I limped slowly around while my hamstring was healing, I decided from now on, not to use gravity as a tool as I went about my home repairs. But the plywood worked, and I could stop worrying about what would come in at night.

~ ~ ~

My rats began to stink. Dead rats – lord do they have a particular odor. But they weren't eating my sweet rolls anymore.

I could still hear things in the attic at night. I assumed it was possums that would come for the warmth of the wood burner that heated the ceiling. But the dust they made come through the ceiling and would get into my bed.

That problem was easy to solve. I had a short, four-step ladder, so I got my plastic and my T-50 stapler and with a lot of overhead effort, I plasticized the ceiling. No more dust and lord knows what else from the critters. Yuck.

With the plastic in place, I noticed more warmth made it into the two west rooms, which gave me an idea. I would put plastic on all the ceilings, and before the next winter, I would tackle the walls. Problem solved – or it seemed solved at the time. But it caused another problem – it held the heat in. Good in winter, not so good in the summer.

I had hopes of a garden but the cows were still here and I didn't want to plant a garden-full of what would become cow food if they got into it. Unfortunately, the owner was having trouble with fence boundaries on his new pasture and needed to leave them a little longer. Oh well.

Big Ugly continued to come around and I was really glad he had been polled because of his love affair with my truck. I could imagine him slinging his head back and forth and slicing my truck up with his horns and his huge strength. Thankfully, that was one thing that wasn't a problem.

Time began to slip by. I didn't have as many bad days. The depression began to lift and I was thinking more clearly. And I knew I had to get a handle on my eating habits. I basically existed on sweet rolls and canned meat. So I made myself cast-iron-skillet cornbread on my outdoor stove.

I also had a big Dutch oven and was learning to manipulate the wind when I cooked. If I needed more heat I blocked the wind. If I needed less heat to cook slow and easy, I let more wind get at the fire.

One day I wanted cake, a chocolate cake, which I loved, and not one of those store-bought things. I hadn't had real, homemade chocolate cake in a long time and decided I was going to make myself one. But the problem was, how? I didn't have an oven.

I got my best cast iron pan – my slicker I called it – and greased and floured it just like I normally would if I was going to bake it in an oven. Then I mixed the cake, poured the batter in the pan, and put it on my stove. In about ten minutes I could tell she was cooking. Woo hoo!

Near the end, I put the Dutch oven lid on the pan and voilà, a few minutes later I had a chocolate cake. It was a little crispy on the bottom and had picked up the oak flavor like the coffee did, but it was good, real good. And I'd solved another problem – how to bake over an open fire.

It took a while, but I learned to cook on a stove that was at the mercy of nature. I cooked out there in the cold, the wind, in rain, in the blistering Texas heat, and whatever came.

Along with the Dutch oven and my slicker, I had a huge skillet. I'd fry a whole chicken up, eat some, and put the leftovers in a baggie and into the ice chest I had found at a yard sale on one of my wandering trips. If you don't already know, yard sales are great places to find cheap stuff, especially if you come across one of someone who moved to the country and then discovered it wasn't quite the carefree life they imagined and were selling all the stuff they'd never again use once they moved back to the city.

Of all the things I picked up along the way, the ones I used the most were some heavy duty packing pads, the kind used for shipping furniture. I got two of them and used them to cover the ice chest. They were great insulators and kept ice for much longer times. They were a dollar apiece.

I mentioned before that it took years to straighten out Jim's estate. With all the paperwork going back and forth, I decided I needed a mailbox at the end of the road. The postman had given me my address and now I needed a mail box. As usual, Middle Son showed up and as usual, I had a project for him. He did a good job, too!

Mail was one of my greatest comforts. I ordered every catalog I could and had *Backwoods Home* and *Countryside* coming. I wrote letters to pen pals and waited for books to come. I worked hard every day but the evenings were mine.

I read everything I could and discovered the odds of my making it here were against me. By all rights, I shouldn't be surviving this life. I was a woman, alone and isolated, living in primitive conditions. I should have already turned tail and run, or died, or gotten hurt. But here I was.

There's something in the human spirit that, if we let it, drives us to overcome hardships, helps us learn new skills, and helps us to survive and even prosper against all the odds. Many of you reading this will know what I mean. But for those who don't, it all boils down to *don't despair, don't quit, don't back up, and never, ever stop dreaming.*

~ ~ ~

The weather warmed quickly and time was running out on my truck. If I didn't pay it off soon, I knew the repo man would be showing up to take it back. So I called my Oldest and asked him to take up the payments. But I needed something to drive, which would be a problem.

He got his credit union to loan him the money to pay off what was still owed on the truck. But he couldn't borrow enough to buy out my equity in it. It was a nice vehicle. Jim and I bought it when he first got sick, before we moved to San Antonio, because we had to drive so far and so often for him to get his treatments. Even though it was a few years old, now, it was in great shape. We always took good care of it because it was, literally, our lifeline. I was sad that I had to part with the truck, but I figured it was better to lose my equity in it and let my son have it than to lose it all to a mortgage company. And he did give me, in trade, an old Chevy pickup he had so I could get around.

When Oldest Son showed up, I quickly got over the disappointment of the trade of trucks when I saw, in the back, an old, free-standing cabinet he'd salvaged from a Missouri Pacific Railroad house they were moving to a historic district. The monster was heavy, but we managed to lug it into my Someday Kitchen.

It was just what I needed. The bottom shelves had doors I could close things up in and it had four open shelves on the top. I'd been living out of boxes for so long, it would be great to get my pans, dishes, glasses, and other kitchen stuff out of them. It was wonderful! But it was so heavy, if it ever fell over, it could have hurt me bad or killed me. So he'd brought a hammer and nails to fasten it to the wall.

At least, that was the plan.

The first nail pinged and jumped backwards. Like the siding outside, this, too, was a tough old wall. He kept trying until he found a spot that would take a nail – just one – and sparks flew with each swing.

That old cabinet was a great joy and served me well for a long time. I took it with me years later when I finally moved on. I still have it, as well as the old wood burner, which has almost rusted down to nothing now, and my old enamel coffee pots, my axe, and my last pair of leather gloves. They are my only reminders of my time in the ole house.

Next he showed me the tricks to the old truck, and boy was it tricky. The distributor would slip and it would die, but never when you were on the road – only at a stop light, with a dozen cars and trucks behind me. That was fun.

The boys were headed to Missouri on a job. That kinda scared me because they would be a long way off, but I had plenty to keep me busy.

~ ~ ~

I had been notified I was needed in Dallas for an affidavit in the long-ago lawsuit Jim filed, so I drove to Houston to borrow my son's little step-side Chevy. He'd taken a company truck to the Missouri job.

The round-trip took two days, and I was exhausted when I got back. I was grieved at the meanness of corporate lawyers and was drained emotionally and physically. I'd forgotten how noisy cities are and didn't realize just how much the opposite it was at my new home, and how used to the peace and quiet I'd become.

When I got back to Houston, I rested a bit, then gathered up Tippy and headed back out to my home in my new old truck. As I was driving down the road, I saw a big pile of gutter and stuff in a trash pile, so I wheeled over, thinking all they can do is say no.

Knocking on the door was kinda scary. You never know who's on the other side. A man answered the door and I asked him if it was possible for me to have the gutter at the curb.

"Sure," he said, "but ya gotta take it all."

Oh Lord, what had I done? I saw an opportunity to get some free stuff for the house, but he saw an opportunity to have someone clean up and haul away that pile for free. What I needed was a plan.

As I mentioned before, I always have plenty of rope in the truck, so I put the tailgate down. The long pieces went in first, then the shorter pieces and elbows and such went on top. Then I tied it all down. It was a strange-looking mess, but I was glad to have it. To this day I smile about that adventure.

Old Tippy wagged her tail when I got in the truck. I told her I just got us a way to build a water catchment system and she acted like she knew what I was talking about, which was more than I knew because I had no idea how I was going to get the gutter nailed to the ole house below the roof.

But I did know how I was going to build one for the Cistern.

~ ~ ~

When I finally arrived home, I unloaded my treasure-trash.

About twenty feet from the cistern was a partial shed. I think at one time it had been used to keep wood dry. The years and cows had knocked much of it down, but it still had two sides standing. The siding and roof for the shed were made of salvaged, open-end tin that was about twelve feet long.

I started my fire for coffee and began to think, wondering what kind of roof-drop I needed to catch water.

In the meantime, it was nice and warm, so I opened up the house. I had to find sticks to hold the windows up. As I worked on what I guessed had been the living room, I heard a little mewing, so I went out front and listened but the grass was so tall I couldn't see anything.

As I walked toward the road, I saw the source, a tiny white kitten. And there by its side was a collie puppy about six to eight weeks old. I wondered who could have thrown away these babies. It was a wonder the coyotes hadn't heard them and eaten them. I was furious, even as my heart went out to the poor babies, so I gathered them up and took them into the house.

They were starving to death, shaking and afraid. I gave the kitten some canned milk and wet down some of Tippy's dog food for the pup. Weeks later, the kitten went to a home of a relative, but the collie puppy stayed with me for some time. I called him Charlie Brown, and if I went into town, he and Tippy both kept me company. One day I asked, "You want to go to town, Charlie?" and he hopped right into the truck. From then on he was called Downtown Charlie Brown.

Years later, he went to Minnesota with my Oldest Son where he lived to be seventeen years old. After he left, I missed him, so I wrote a cute story – from a dog's point of view – about Charlie Brown and I having a conversation about a wedding and Barbie dolls and other things. Oldest Son would marry a woman with little girls and I discussed Charlie Brown's new family with him in the letter, explaining about little girls and Barbies and what marriage was. It was a funny letter and I wish it hadn't been lost years ago.

I had boxes, so I made the babies a bed and they stayed together. Tippy was spayed and never had a litter, but she took over the nursery. As I trained them to potty outside, she would monitor. I was glad for her, that she had something to do besides worry about me. She was with me every step of the way and these little ones gave her comfort. Tippy was the dog everyone liked, gentle and loving, but an avid hunter.

Through the years, I would find many dogs that had been dumped off. Some, I adopted and was able to get back in shape but others were so sick and would have been a danger to the ones I had. It was so very hard to put them down – a hard, but necessary and ultimately kind thing their owners should have done – but my life was far from easy and I had to make some tough decisions. But it was always so sad.

But back to my water shed.

I needed to prop the shed back up if I was going to use the roof to catch water, so I headed out to my dump where there were some lengths of plastic pipe that were about the right length.

I wasn't exactly thrilled when it was done, but I was proud that I had thought it out and come up with an idea to save precious water. At one time the pictures were published in Countryside magazine. I sent them to *Backwoods Home*, too, but they didn't publish them. This was in the early years and I'm sure they had plenty of more important projects to publish. I was disappointed, but I loved the magazine and got over it. *[Publisher's Note: Generally, magazines do not accept previously-published material.]*

The shed looked like a four-legged spider, sloped to the front, since there were holes in the tin and holes where the gutter had been attached to the roof. After I had dug holes for new poles and got them steadied, I wired the gutter to the shed using the holes. I had to wire pieces of the gutter together to slope it to the cistern.

The water shed with the gutter leading to the cistern. To the right is the dishwashing area.

I couldn't test it to see how it would flow until it rained, so I waited patiently while getting other things done. When the day finally came that it did rain, I was out in it, watching and adjusting the down-slope on the pipe.

I quickly realized I would have to block up the middle. The weight of the water was making it sag. That's when I had another idea. If I could stabilize the pipes leading to the cistern, I could caulk the seams and eliminate leakage. My brain was working again and throughout the rest of the day, I worked on the pipe. I can't say I always knew exactly what I was doing. I wasn't an engineer, after all, but I figured storms blowing through would quickly show me the weak points in my system that needed fixing.

You can't know how I good I felt about the accomplishment. It's impossible to live without water and I quickly learned how to collect and purify my water and survive. Maintaining my water source was my top priority. During long droughts, the old cistern would literally save my life, and maybe also the oak tree's life, which used it as a sippy cup. A rain barrel on the corner of the house fed my personal solar shower water and at one time, I had to purify it to be able to drink it.

A funny note – sometime during all this, a frog, a long skinny green frog, fell into the cistern and stayed there for a long time. I felt sorry for him. He wouldn't let me fish him out, so I threw a small chunk of a 2x4 into it so he didn't have to tread water all the time. As it turned out, he kept the bugs cleaned out, so the arrangement worked for me.

I learned to live in peace with my creature neighbors, except for the scorpions. There were a lot of them and one winter, they would sting me eight times.

~ ~ ~

Through the years, the Chinaberry tree had grown so large, it pushed against the roof on the west side, causing it to leak and the leaking roof had started rotting the wood. Naturally, termites began to take over that side of the house and the scorpions came to eat them and, in the winter, to stay warm from the heat of the house. I didn't even realize they were there until one dropped in my bed and stung me on the arm.

There were two kinds – the long, skinny ones and the short, fat ones. The sting of the skinny ones wasn't as potent as that of the fat ones. One of the fatties stung me on the foot once as I fed my little animal crew and I stayed up all night suffering from it. The venom caused my heart to race as I shook uncontrollably. As the night wore on, I kept telling myself I'd whip them, one way or another. Then it occurred to me that they'd survived people like me for millions of years. What was I going to do against them?

It turned out, the old Postman would tell me what to do, and cedar became my friend.

~ ~ ~

After I bought the two rain barrels, I'd watched where the rain ran off the tin roof of the house and set them on the corners on the east side. But it was a fickle catchment system. If we had a gentle rain, the runoff landed in the barrels, but if it rained hard, it missed.

I had to figure out a way to attach some of my salvaged gutter to the eves of the house so I could direct the water into the barrels no matter how hard it rained. I hated to have to borrow or ask for help, but I had no choice. I would have to go see my Postman neighbor.

I hopped in my truck and took off down the road. Yep, despite the cattleman's warning, I forgot about the mud. I had no idea how the old truck would do in the boggy mess, so I dropped her down a gear and my goodness, she took off like a bull elephant. The mud didn't bother her one bit. It did drag her tail pipe off, but that was no problem. I'd pick it up on the way back. It was too hot to handle now, anyway.

If you've never driven in the country after a good rain, you probably can't appreciate how I felt that first time. I wish I could describe it better, with the overhanging oaks, the wooden-bridges, the creek bubbling along. All I can, say is that it was serene and oddly quiet, despite the truck engine.

When I got to The Postman's house, the woodpile work was going full force. It took a minute to find the old fellow. He was in his early seventies, but totally active. I think he kept himself busy because of his wife's recent passing, kinda like me. As the years went by, I learned he had many money-making ideas. Unfortunately, his Youngest Son had just as many money-spending ideas.

I told him what I needed to do and apologized for having to ask, but I needed a cordless drill – did he have one?

He said, "Let me come help you." Then he loaded a ladder, some strapping, some screws, and his drill – a big one, nice and powerful. We were gonna need it.

Off we went down the road. I stopped and picked up the tail-pipe, mud and all.

When we reached my place, we got set up. It was a good thing he brought that strapping. It saved my bacon, because the wood was so tough it probably would have shattered if we tried to screw the gutter directly onto it.

Maybe I should have used his ladder and he used mine because he was tall and I had to stand on the top of my short ladder, stretching to the limits of what my five-foot, five-inch frame would allow. It took us a good 2 hours. The tough old wood ate at the batteries, but in the end, we had my rain gutter up. Now, all I had to do was monitor the rain to get the most out of my gutters.

By this time it had warmed up. Spring had gone by so quickly that first year. I missed the cool nights and nice mild days. In the summer it would be so hot, firing up the tubs was too much work just to bathe, so I'd take a rain-water bath, or use my solar shower I had bought from Walmart.

With the heat would come the offer of a job that thrilled me, exasperated me, and in the end, almost killed me.

My old home was taking shape.

My Postman friend came down one day and said he didn't want to embarrass me but did I need some furniture? His son and daughter-in-law had bought some new stuff and were going to toss the old if nobody wanted it.

I told him, "Let me come take a look." Like there was even a possibility I was going to turn it down.

It was a brown plaid set, a sofa and chair, and it was way too big for their little house.

"Yep," I said. "I'll take it." So he helped me load it and off we went.

Remembering how old the house is, you'll understand the doors weren't all that wide. We fought that old couch for a while before we finally just manhandled it in. Voilà! I was making progress. I had a chair to sit in and a couch for company. What company? I shouldn't have even thought about it.

I thanked him and off he went.

One thing I learned quickly was not to get all syrupy with folks. They don't trust that. Someone does you a good turn, you just thank them. Maybe stop by with a home-baked pie or some muffins one day.

Not that they'd expect it. I know he didn't. But the day would come when I would be able to help fight a fire that would almost get his house and the woodpile; a fire caused by some careless weekend warriors, a bane to us backwoods folks.

The living room. The boom box radio was my only source of outside news.

I had been cleaning his house every Monday and his daughter-in-law asked me to do hers. I did. One time. It took me two weeks of chasing to get my money, and it wasn't even from her. One day when he stopped with my mail, the old Postman asked me if she had paid me, yet. I hesitated, then told him no. He took out his wallet and paid me on the spot.

I would later learn that she was a big problem when it came to money. She'd let people work for a couple of weeks, telling them they had to sell some wood first, so they could pay them, then she'd fire them, unpaid. She and the son couldn't even go into the small town seven miles away. There were too many people they owed money to, people who were mad and threatening them and I don't blame them. It's not right to treat people that way, to take advantage of them the way they did.

I bought more books. Reading was my great joy. And about this time, with the spring over and summer hitting full force, I learned just how hot the ole house could get and I would find a cool place in the back of the fifty acres to pray and to meditate. It would bring me more

47

connection to my God. Prayer mellowed my mind and gave me great courage when I needed it. And I did need it.

~ ~ ~

My supply of kerosene for my lamps was getting low, so I headed to the feed store. As soon as I arrived, I noticed there had been some changes. There was a new guy behind the register and I realized it bothered me. I also realized that even in the short time I'd lived here, I'd begin to think like others who lived along The Road. I had begun to detest change.

At first people were stand-offish to him – boy I understood that – but they, and I, soon warmed up. He and his wife were likeable people.

Through the years, as they upgraded and added new products, he would be there to help me, laugh with me, and be someone I could trust.

I checked out after getting my kerosene and one of the best investments I ever made – a pair of good leather gloves. There was a cord that let me pull them in tight against my wrist to keep dirt and stuff out and they protected my hands when handling critters and when I gathered dead-fall firewood.

Off I went back to the house. When I passed my teen neighbor riding his horse, I knew I would have a visitor in a bit, and I did.

The boy stopped and talked a long time. His mother had left them – I suppose for greener pastures. I had to tell him he had to live his life and let his parents fight it through. He was such a good kid, and seemed to grow more with every passing day. Sometimes things are hard to talk about and it's hard to know the right thing to say, especially to a boy his age, but we talked, and I did my best to muddle through.

After he left, I fixed myself some black tea and honey and went to read on the front porch. That's when the humming birds started diving into my tea. As I sat very still they would perch on the edge of my coffee cup and drink. They were all different colors and some were tiny babies. Amazing!! I needed some feeders – they were on the list. I already knew how to mix the food for them from reading one of my books. By the time I was done, I had humming bird feeders all around my front porch.

It was a good day.

~ ~ ~

It grew hotter and hotter, and I had to think about leaving the doors open. I needed a cross breeze. Lord that ole house was hot. The tin roof turned her into an adult-sized Easy Bake oven and I was the roast! I would get desperately hot before I finally got brave enough to leave them open at night.

The guy that owned the cattle came one weekend to get them. He took the girls first and the bull last. He mooed and snorted all day and came to the front looking for them. He seemed puzzled at where his buddy the truck was.

He was normally friendly enough, gentle even, but a bull is a bull and I didn't get too close to him, except for that night he tried the back-porch sleeping thing that caused so much damage.

I would really miss the cattle. It was almost comforting having them there. But I wouldn't miss the mess they created in my backyard kitchen. And after that day, I wouldn't see the cow guy again. I missed him too.

I had fished salt water all my life, so I knew how to do that, but had never fresh-water fished. I learned that worm fishing is a whole lot squishier than using squid or shrimp, but I got over it.

Now that the cows were gone, I'd go back to the pond to fish a couple of times a week. I would take my butt-bucket – the milk crate I used for a table, and catch six to eight pan fryers, perch mostly. I knew how to gut and gill fish and scale them. I had taught my boys. The bass I threw back. They were too small so I figured I'd let 'em grow.

I cleaned them at the pond, then came home, fired up my big cast iron skillet, and had a gourmet meal – fried up crisp perch. Life was good.

One evening as I sat on the porch cooling off just before twilight, I caught something moving out of the corner of my left eye. I sat very still. It was a female wolf with a pup. She was a big beautiful animal. The pup looked like it was half shepherd but I didn't know if that happened and figured I'd have to ask someone one more dumb question. She had a running walk and didn't falter as she passed me. And the dogs were strangely silent. She paid me no attention, just trotted easily by about ten to fifteen feet from me. There would be times during the next couple of years that I would see her standing way off, watching.

I put out dog food thinking if she eats, she won't be killing calves. I don't know if it worked.

Life was taking shape, despite the unbearable heat.

~ ~ ~

It was moving time. I thought if I just opened the back door and the windows in the front of the house, I would get a breeze. I took my bed and chest into the east side room and tried leaving the back door open. You can probably guess the problems that caused. The rats were gone, but the mice and snakes were not. One would give me the fright of a lifetime.

The next morning I fired up the outdoor stove. I had vowed to eat well in the mornings and I wanted pancakes with my coffee.

I had the coffee simmering and the skillet heating. It wouldn't take but a few minutes to mix the batter. I reached for the flour, knowing exactly where it was, and wondered why it was cold and felt like that. As I turned around to look, a BIG rat snake started to uncoil. They're non-poisonous, but Lord can they give you a scare. He was waiting for a mouse.

I didn't want to kill him. There was no reason to. It wasn't a threat to me physically. So I grabbed the broom to slip under him and move him/her outdoors.

Snakes shouldn't hiss at me. I stepped out to the back porch, grabbed my very sharp hoe, and tried one more time to remove it. NOPE!!

It's not all that easy to nicely kill a snake in the kitchen. By the time I got through with that stubborn snake, it was in about 40 pieces and I wasn't aware of the mess I was making! Geezzz! There was flour, sugar, and oatmeal all over the place along with pots and pans and anything else that got in the way of me and the snake.

By now, I really needed that cup of coffee. Forget the pancakes. Holy crap! What drama! I had to laugh. It's a good thing I wasn't afraid of snakes, but it did take a couple of days before I stopped being spooked every time I went into the kitchen, and to get all the flour, oats, and sugar cleaned up.

~ ~ ~

Now that the cows were gone, I could finally go to the back of the lot to practice with my shotgun.

I found an old bottomless bucket in the dump. I hung it so it would be chest-high on a six-foot-tall man. I didn't want to practice wounding. I wanted to practice stopping my enemy, period. So with ammo in hand, I took my .20ga. and started shooting. At 25 feet, 50 feet, 75 feet, and then at 100 feet I got different patterns and saw what my ammo would do. Scary.

I liked the 50- to 75 foot shots best, but I chose the 25- and 50-foot shots to practice the most. I figured if a bad guy was any closer, he'd be stopped right there and there'd be no need to call a doctor. But the further the shot, the more I would need to practice. I spent a lot of time back there practicing both shooting and a five-shot reload. I needed to be able to do it quickly.

Time after time, shot after shot, reload after reload, I practiced. Shoot, reload, shoot, reload, and, of course, without a clip. Just single-shell reloads. It took time, but at last I felt pretty much able to defend myself and carried the old shotgun everywhere.

With all the critters around, I wasn't keen on having to struggle to get the gun out of its case, so instead, I put an old sock over the muzzle to keep dirt out. The silly pistol would only sting a big muscled up guy, but I kept that around, too.

All the practicing kinda upset the nearest neighbor. He called the old deputy. When he showed up, I took him back and showed him what I had been doing, not because I thought I had to justify anything to my neighbor, but to be friendly with the officer. He knew about the break-in I had and about the terrible death of Zipper the calf. He looked at the setup and didn't say a word, just got back in his car and left.

That was the end of that.

The next day, I heard a tractor out front. Since the cows were gone, the weeds and brush had taken over and my neighbor with the black Ford came with his brush hog to help get it all off the meadow. He also mowed around the house. When he was done, the yard looked so nice. From then on, I kept it mowed with an old twenty-two inch cut mower I brought with me. I mowed at least once a month because the Bahia Grass was tough to mow if you let it get out of hand. It was a big chore, but I was physically up to the job.

It was a relief to be able to walk around without looking for snakes. I also could see to the tree lines and I got so used to every bush and flower, I automatically knew if someone or something had been there.

~ ~ ~

The Lady with the lake cottage came by to get her key because they had sold the place. She was feeling better and told me if I ever needed anything to call her. I thanked her for the work. It had been a payday that I would miss.

Sunday morning as I sat on the porch, I knew I would have to find work, or something to make money. It was too far for the old truck to travel round-trip each day to try Huntsville, and living this far out had its limitations, but I wasn't really worried or scared. I had reached a calm, a trust. My prayers and meditation had paid off so far. I had faith again.

There was a time when I felt I had lost it. I had prayed so hard for Jim's life to be spared, but he continued to get worse and I felt God had abandoned me. I know now that He had directed my path here, because if I hadn't had this trial and all its problems to occupy me, I would have spun off into madness. I had spent two years with a dead man...well...a man who was dying a little more each day. It was a terrible thing to watch happen, especially to someone I loved, and I didn't think I would make it through. But I did and now here I was, figuring out how to survive.

It dawned on me that morning that I knew how to survive. It was in my DNA. I just had to let it loose, to go with what came naturally. I suddenly felt relaxed, in my element. I can remember thanking God for my trials and tribulations because I had grown and matured in my spirit.

And how I loved this hateful ole house I called home.

~ ~ ~

The Postman stopped and honked with a certified letter from the probate lawyer. He asked how it was going and I said fine. He just shook his head.

I remembered the scorpions and asked him how I could get rid of them. I also told him about the termites and how they had taken over rotting parts of the chinaberry side. He explained the scorpions had come for the termites and told me to come down to his place later, after he got in, and he would give me some cedar shavings.

I said, "OK," wondering why I needed cedar. I thought it must be an old-time remedy I hadn't heard of. As time passed, I would learn there were a lot of things I hadn't heard of.

He told me cedar disorients the scorpions and they starve to death. He also said they were blind and were heat and movement seekers, which made sense to me. I hadn't looked that close at them. The next time, I would. (Shiver. Geezzz I hated them.)

I drove to his place and as I rounded the last curve, I had to slam on my brakes. There was a huge, black bull standing in the road in the shade. I almost didn't see him in time. I would later learn this bull was a fence jumper, tear-downer, and all round pest. He had a keen sense of smell, to put it nicely, and was headed to the lady cows when he decided to take a rest. He didn't charge or seem mean, but a bull is a bull and is unpredictable. I eased around him. This would not be my last encounter with him.

When I got to The Postman's place, he was waiting and told me to follow him. He took me to a large metal building full of equipment from heaven, if you're a craftsman. He was making coffee tables out of cedar. He also had jewelry boxes and little stools and was starting a cedar chest for his young granddaughter. Wow, a multi-talented gentleman!

He got a box and handed me a broom and told me to sweep up the shavings and dust, then go home and put it in a quart-size spray bottle and let it sit overnight or longer. When I was ready to use it, I should shake it good and spray around baseboards and hidey places. I had enough chips and dust to eventually spray around the base of the house.

Shortly after spraying, I found five, dead, black-widow spiders. Now that did scare me. I had read in one of my books, that in the spring, when they are hatching their young, they are vicious attackers.

I thanked him and on my way out, I looked into the three-sided barn. At one time, it stored farm equipment. Now it held wood splitters.

I saw how the logs outside were spray painted every twenty-two inches and cut on those painted lines with chain saws. The cut pieces (butts) were then stacked for the guys on the splitters to bust into wedge shaped pieces.

They had a long table set up with a Saran wrap-type film to wrap the short butts into small bundles which were then stacked on pallets. They had to be stacked right, very snug. Then the whole pallet was shrink wrapped.

I would learn in later days that the pallets weighed from 1200- to 1400 pounds, depending on how green the wood was. Per Forestry regulations, the only woods used were hardwoods. Pine was too dangerous to burn in stoves and fireplaces because of tar build-up in chimneys. The tar could ignite and the whole house could burn down.

There weren't but 3 guys splitting the short butts. One sat using the ugliest splitter I had ever seen. It wasn't shiny and new like Tractor Supply had, oh no. This was an old 40 tonner and would become my special tool one day in a race to have 24 pallets a day ready to be loaded when The Postman's son returned from his previous load.

The other 2 splitters were 25 tonners – lightweights compared to the old one. The guys were Mexicans. I would, in the end, have the best crew anyone could ask for. By the way, everyone was documented. They had to be, as they weren't just checked by Immigration officials, but by local cops and Game Wardens, too!

I knew I would work here. I told The Postman, "If you need help, let me know," then added, "I really need the work."

~ ~ ~

The days became miserably hot. The dead rats in the attic and walls stunk to high heaven.

My ritual was to fill my tubs in the mornings and start fires under them and my back-yard cook stove. By the time coffee boiled and I had a cup, the air would already be warm-to-hot and humid

The collie puppy, Charlie Brown, was coming along nicely, but I had to watch him around the cistern. I wanted to build a woodpecker-wire cover for it so I wouldn't have to worry about him falling in. That went on my list. When I called in to the kids next time, I would have someone bring me a roll of it.

On rare nights, I could dial up Alex Jones on my battery-powered radio. He would scare me so bad. That guy would have had me paranoid and hiding in the bushes if I listened very much. I also picked up a few Dallas football games.

Listening to the radio in these trees was as challenging as using a cell phone would become the day I finally got one. I had hung a wire to use as an antenna on some nails that had been there on the porch for years, and would have to twist and turn it just to keep tuned in.

Summer was in full bloom, but I needed work bad. My money was running on near-empty. Thank God for canned milk and Vienna sausages. I had bought as much canned stuff as I could afford, but what I wouldn't give for a glass of sweet tea.

Back toward the end of the month, I was feeling a little down. I was reading and had the doors and windows open, hoping for a breeze, but the air was so still.

Ole Tippy began to whine. She wasn't usually a whiner or a barker, but now she paced and made sounds at the door.

Oh heck. I figured something, or someone, was going on outside. It was getting very dark, so I got the gun and thought, *now what.* I also had my Maglite (my up close equalizer) and stepped out the door. Tippy shot across the yard. I called her back and she came but she walked around me like she was guiding me. There was a cardboard box by the gate. Leery of what was in the box, I approached it slowly.

When had they set it there? I had only heard one truck and it had stopped a-ways up the road. I'd assumed it was a potty break, but now I knew what they had done.

The box had four pretty good sized puppies in it. Their eyes were still closed. *Now what do I do? I keep 'em, of course.* They were Rottweilers, small black and brown bundles, and they looked like their mother or something had chewed them up and they had worms in their wounds. It was a horrible sight. I had some tincture of violet and used cotton balls to put it on their wounds. I ended up with the stuff all over me thanks to the wriggling, resisting puppies. Thankfully, it killed the worms.

I knew the pups had to be hungry and that I needed to feed them, so I got some canned milk and used the eye dropper from some earache medicine I had. It was difficult and took a while, but I got them each fed, supervised by Tippy, of course. I decided to make things easier and buy a baby bottle to feed them when I went to town.

Their wounds broke my heart. I made a little tub of warm water, bathed their wounds and dried them, and wrapped them up after using some of the spray can of wound dressing I'd bought for myself. It was animal grade 'cause it was cheaper. It was an offshoot of tincture of violet.

During the night, I got up to feed the wee newborns, hoping they would make it, but by morning one was dead. Two more would die in the next few days. I called the one who made it Dog, as he became a big, bad looking dog. Though he was big and muscled up, he was gentle as a lamb and would find a buddy in my young friend and neighbor the horse rider, who fell in love with him and would come help me feed him.

Months later, when he would ride his horse by the house, he would whistle and off Dog would go. It was a blessing for the boy. He had so little love or care from his family. His younger brother had moved in with his mother, but my young friend stayed to finish high school, lettering in football and making great grades.

The day came when the boy turned into a man, graduated from high school, and went to Houston to live and work, and go to college. He asked for Dog and, with a sad heart, I said yes. Anything for a friend.

Sometimes life is just like that. He...we...got past the bad times together. We spent many hours on my front porch, talking, letting his horse graze. At times, he would ride his horse to my place in the morning, catch the bus there, and let his horse graze the pasture all day. He didn't know I was grieving. He just gave me simple friendship while asking nothing in return. We both won. He never knew he helped me past some bad times just by being there.

~ ~ ~

I turned my bath tub into a washing machine with hot water and a commode plunger for an agitator. I'd soak 'em, wring them out, and rinse them in the tub.

I had plenty of trees, so I had good clotheslines. And I had enough to wear so I didn't need to wash as often. When I did, it took all day, but I didn't complain. It was saving me a bundle on gas and going to nasty Laundromats.

In the winters it was different. I wore heavy sweats and they were so heavy it was too much trying to wring them out so I had to go to the in-town laundry.

These trips to town left me uneasy at times, watching people and their behavior, their disregard for others, the vulgar public language, and blatant drug use. I couldn't wait to get back to safety behind my gate. Really, though, it was only the illusion of safety, but at least I had a chance there in my haven from the world, for the moment anyway.

So many small things that we take for granted on-grid can be a major problem off grid. I learned to cook beans and stews in smaller portions and to deal with the heat and no fridge. I knew food wouldn't keep in the heat. I learned to build a small fire on one end of my outside stove and when cooking was done, I'd move it to the cooler side to keep warm.

My pups were doing ok. At night I would laugh at their antics. If they got too rough and got mad at each other, Tippy would step in and separate them, just like a momma dog would. She was something else. Dog didn't get to bond with his mother, so she wasn't able to give him his social skills, but Tippy seemed to know how to do that.

The seasonal creek that ran across the property was home to lots of frogs of every kind as well as other creatures. Tippy would hunt along the creek, disturbing their sunbathing. That's where she got her first snake bite.

I heard something fall on the front porch and I looked and she was down, panting hard. I grabbed her and saw the swelling. *Oh my God.* She was getting in bad shape fast. I laid her down, jumped in the truck, and drove like a maniac to The Postman's house.

I ran up and pounded on his door. "What do I do?"

He said, "Nothing. Let her alone. Offer water, but let her system try to work out the poison"

I didn't know what kind of snake bit her, a cottonmouth, a rattlesnake, or a copperhead. We had all three around there, bad. The only lasting effect I could see was with her eyes; she seemed not to have her vision of old. And once in a while she would shiver.

Lord have mercy. I felt so helpless. If you have ever prayed over an animal, you know the feeling. I begged God for her life. She was such a huge part of my life. Weighing only twelve to fifteen pounds, she was a lion to me.

For three days I watched her shiver, glassy eyed. I soothed her by talking to her and took the eye-dropper and gently fed her water. The puppies whined and somehow I think they gave her the fight she needed. On the 4th day, she tried to stand, so I mashed her up some Vienna sausages and she ate them! Man, I was cheering and the puppies and kitten watched her ever so quietly. That night, they all curled up together.

When the old Postman came to see how she was doing, I told him she made it. He said "I don't see how" but I knew. She couldn't leave us, me and the pups. She had to watch over us. And she did, for almost seventeen years. And when she couldn't raise herself up to follow me any longer, I had to do the unthinkable. To this day, I can picture the tall, gangly girl wagging her tail as if to say let's go!

Tippy, snake-bit and near death

Tippy also had a standing appointment with skunks...oh, yeah...and no matter how much I fussed at her, she never got the message to just leave 'em alone. I bought the cheapest tomato juice I could find and oh, how she hated the tomato juice baths.

~ ~ ~

Tippy had her shots – rabies and 7/1, *[Distemper, Parvovirus, Adenovirus, Hepatitis, Parainfluenza, and 2 strains of Lepto –Ed.]* Now I needed to get the pups wormed and their early baby shots. Add to the to-do list:

* Shots – Daughter could give them. She raised doxies.

* Son – Bring woodpecker wire.

It was so very hot, but in my current mindset, it was a way of life. I wore shorts and tanks and tennis shoes, always.

From the time you open your eyes off-grid you are busy and thinking of ways to make things easier/better. If it rained, my cooking stove wasn't much good. Heating water took on a new challenge. I had found a way to keep wood dry. Warm as it was, showers were solar.

I never in all the years used a paper plate or Styrofoam cup. I used dishes. I hated plastic. It was a thing with me. Living out in the wild like I did didn't mean I ate garbage or off the floor. The house may have been old, and in tough shape, but it wasn't a cave.

I hand sewed some pillows for my couch and I liked a tablecloth on my table – when I wasn't using it to make biscuits. I needed that homey touch.

For the coming Christmas, I would decorate my tree with pine-cones I found, all different sizes, as I walked over the fifty acres collecting. The tree was a cedar I found in the back of the lot. It was a very special Christmas, my first off-grid. I coated each pine cone with glue that dried clear and sprinkled them with glitter, then glued a ribbon to the big end for hanging. It was a very pretty tree.

Routine set in. It was the middle of June. I was very fit from being so active. Not that I had a choice. There was always something to do.

Life changed early one morning, before daylight. I was yanked awake by a horn honking. I jumped up thinking it was one of the kids, but nope it was The Postman asking me if I wanted a job. WOW!!! Yes I did.

So began the most unusual thing I had ever done. This job would start a part of my life that I loved. You would shake your head if you could have seen the setup. Primitive doesn't quite explain it. And you probably wouldn't have believed that anyone would love this alternately freezing cold and boiling heat, sitting over a fumy, hot-exhaust machine doing dirty, dangerous, aggravating, nerve-testing kinda work. But I did and it would come to redefine my physical condition, my attitude, my character, and my very being.

It would be rocky start, working in the woodpile, but it would be a job I mastered. For the next 6-1/2 years, I would run a wood splitter, making little sticks out of logs. And for 6-1/2 years, it would keep me in the small comforts of food and clothes and animal food for all the critters abandoned or that I found. I would be mad, glad, proud, aggravated, and worn out, but always working.

My life changed each year from the middle of April until the 15th of December. It was seasonal work, during which I would have to battle for my money, I would have to fire men, and I would have to hunt for, hire, and transport them, and all the time, keep working the logs.

I changed oil in the splitters, kept track of the gas needed for them, and taught many of the new workers how to split wood without losing fingers or toes. I would come to supervise the chain saws, trying to keep idiots from cutting off a limb. And I would have to make them aware that logs rolling off the fork lift could kill them, and that they should never go in the yard while the fork lift was moving because the logs weren't tied or chained for moving such short distances.

I worked in freezing weather, in the rain, and in the awful summer heat. I fought the mud and found some interesting critters in rotten tree trunks. I figured out tree knots will put a hurtin' on you when you popped them off a hickory or oak butt.

And I met some very interesting people. Some drove lowboys full of cut hickory for our special business. There were folks wanting wood for their barbecues and businesses, and once, some detectives looking for a killer (nope we didn't have him.)

I dug my Mexican workers out of the bushes when INS showed up and fired smart-ass Yankees running from the law who were always pushing their weight around. When they got in my face, they got a surprise. I don't back up and I don't quit. And when I had to come off my splitter to argue with them, I came with a 22 inch piece of oak. They got to walk back to town or ride with the Sheriff. We didn't need or want their attitudes and I certainly wasn't going to put up with it. I would even fight The Postman's daughter-in-law for money to pay my crew. And I would put up with some real egos, chief among them, the owners son, who I called The Ego, but not to his face, of course.

The Postman never called me by my name. His name for me was Hun and he was my go-to guy. He once had a heart-attack on his 160 mile route, finished the route, and then went to the ER. Soon after, he retired, and we began our journey as friends.

~ ~ ~

The morning he asked me to come work for him, I wouldn't get coffee. I told him to let me get dressed and I'd be right there.

I threw some Vienna sausages and crackers in a sack, grabbed a jug of water, my gloves, and my cap, which kept spider webs out of my hair. (Not funny)

I didn't know exactly what I would be doing, but it paid money, and I needed money. I'm a quick study and knew I had the strength to do whatever it was.

When I got down to his house, he showed me my splitter – geezzz a sissy, 25-tonner. Then he rolled a log butt over to me and told me to sit on it. There weren't but two Mexicans there then because it was just daylight. As it turned out, I underestimated the 25-tonners – did they ever fire out some wood!

One came over to show me how to start it, kinda like a lawn mower. (Except when it's cold. Thank God for cans of ether.) But it was warm and we didn't have any trouble. He helped me pile up some log butts. I had noticed they piled them next to the seats, which made sense, so they didn't have to jump up and down each time they finished splitting a log. He showed me how to hold the log butt up against the back, and showed me how to follow the natural cracks in the wood. The first time I popped that wood open, I was amazed. But I knew that I knew how to do it. I liked this job.

My rude awaking came when we didn't knock off at four, five, or even six o'clock. No, we worked 'till dark!!!

I was worried about the pups. I was hungry, my back was killing me, my shins were bruised all up and down both of them, I was grimy and so tired I could hardly move. But I was getting the hang of it, especially the part about getting my shins out of the way.

One more thing. My own butt was raw from sitting on that rough sawed tree butt. Ohhh...my...goodness! My backside felt like it was on fire. I decided I'd have a different butt-bucket tomorrow.

I cringed thinking about my butt boo-boos – man that hurt– but I didn't say a word. Finally, I got home and was relieved to find the pups were okay. Tippy had her legs crossed. She wanted to get out and the pups followed her, but they were also all hungry so I didn't have to chase them to get them back in.

I needed a sitz bath for my sore behind. That kind of friction of sitting on a log all day just ain't right. But I solar showered, fired up the outdoor cook stove, and set an oil lamp between it and my Maglite. Then I made coffee and got out my thermos so I'd have coffee in the morning. I needed it, too.

Sore? I have never before or since been as sore as I was after that first day. I was bruised and hurt in every inch of my body. I could barely get out of bed the next morning.

What was I thinking?

~ ~ ~

When I got to work the next day, I had my plastic milk crate and a pillow to sit on. Oh yeah. No more burning butt for me.

I knew I had to work out my stiffness and sore muscles, that it would take time, and within a week, I was feeling much better. My stamina was better, too. I was getting faster and my pile of split wood was getting higher.

Then the Schoolyard Bully showed up. He was a friend of The Ego and he started piling wood on my side stack. I noticed it was different. The Mexicans looked at me and then each other and I saw they had the kind of wood I had split the day before.

I never in my life got ahold of anything as tough. The logs slipped, folded over, shot out from under the wedge – what the hell had he given me? About that time, out came The Postman and saw what was going on. After a thorough cussing, The Bully got up and walked off. But he would be back. Way too many times I would have to deal with him and his idiot wife and her immature mess. Lord, how many times was it?

Totally puzzled, I asked The Postman what kind of wood it was. It turned out to be elm – wet, red elm. While splitting oak and other hardwoods was pretty straightforward, splitting that elm was like a science project. It had to be done just so.

The Postman showed me how. First you had to slice the edges of the round butt four times to make it square. Then you started slicing off wedges. But because it was a ragged, stringy wood, it didn't split clean like other hardwoods. The Postman got us all small hatchets to keep by our splitters to chop the stringy hateful wedges loose from the butt we were working on. It was the most difficult wood to split. If you have ever tried to cut a sponge with a butter knife, you'll understand what I am talking about.

It would become our go-to wood when we were out of regular hardwoods but green elm was too difficult to split and made a cold, smoky fire so I learned to have the men haul it off to the side to let it dry for a couple of weeks, or even longer, before we split it, and then put it aside again to dry more once it was split.

Elm became our pet peeve, but we had to use it many times, when the oak wasn't coming in.

The days began to go by and, kinda puzzled, I asked when payday was.

"When we make our first load!"

What!!!

I told them I wanted my money every week. I wasn't on vacation. I needed money to live on and I didn't work free.

He told me the Mexicans had agreed. Oh no, I could see it coming.

Having trusted The Postman, I asked him, "By the way, what ya paying me?"

"$7.00 an hour."

Oh my God. But, I had to calm down. I didn't have to worry about clothes. It wasn't but six miles down the road and I'd hang with it until I had some money put back. Years later, that thought would come back to haunt me.

The goal was twenty-four pallets a day. With three people? Good luck. That ain't happening.

I got better and better as I worked. The wood was coming in fairly fast. Later, when we had six to eight splitters going, we couldn't keep wood in the yard.

Our job was to pile the wood deep, so it would be ready for the wrappers every day. We worked from daylight to dark, five to six days a week. And when the season was in full swing, we worked seven days a week.

I wondered why the logs were cut into twenty-two inch butts?

The Postman said they had experimented a lot. Anything longer didn't load on the pallets right and they sold the pallets by how many bundles were on them. Also, too much overhang cut the shrink wrap and they didn't fit in the trailer without hanging up. I was surprised they made it to town (Houston, Huntsville, Katy, etc.) The Ego wrecked three trucks that I know of.

The Ego and his wife were the only ones who slept late. When they did come out, it was mostly to gripe, bitch, fuss, fume, etc., etc.

She may have been a drama queen, but she did it well. She would be dressed with her nails done, her false fanny in place and boobs, too, along with wigs, make up, false eye lashes, and heels – in a woodpile. Geez!

The Mexicans and I breathed a sigh of relief when they left the place, usually around noon.

The Postman usually fussed and fumed when people (Walmart, Krogers, etc.) called about their order saying they could only take deliveries between certain hours on certain days.

He was a regimented man and he couldn't figure out his over-egoed son. I didn't try and would soon enough discover it was a lost cause.

~ ~ ~

There was an old wood burner in the barn where we would later set up the splitters. The place was mostly used on bad weather days, to break the wind or for relief from the sun and heat. The wood burner became our heating and cook stove. The Mexicans and I shared many meals we cooked there. It beat starving to death.

The barn housed a cow operation. The Postman would raise the calves and then sell them when they were about a year old. When the cows were on this side of the pasture, we would have to shovel all the cow patties before we could even begin our work day. Of course the cows got into everything!!!

Meanwhile, at home, my little guys adjusted. The puppies bonded. They were so used to me being there I hated leaving them.

My Oldest Son and his wife and my Middle Son and his girlfriend came out to bring me some things and my daughter-in-law fell in love with the white kitten. My son suggested we build an outhouse. That worked for me. He said next time he came he'd bring plywood. It was a great plan that would turn into a hilarious undertaking.

Before they left, Middle Son's girlfriend made a very stupid mistake – she washed her long hair in my rain barrel. Good grief! I asked her if she wanted to drink out of that barrel. It had never dawned on her that I didn't have running water. We had a good go-round about that. I had to empty the thing, drag the barrel close to the cistern, then scrub it down and bleach it. I was so mad I was livid. Idiot! From then on, I gave fair warning to everybody about my water.

Over time, I would discover that most people didn't leave their city ways behind when they came out to the country. They expected all the amenities they had in town, on-grid.

The weeks rocked on and the weather blazed away. The Postman saw that I was paid. He was always running for chain saw blades, gas, etc., and he always asked if I needed anything. I would give him my list and money.

I began to use the little freezer on his back porch. Now I could take out meat and let it defrost while I was working. Many times we cooked it over the old wood burner or the small barbecue pit that was there. I worked so late there was never time to cook supper. It took too long to fire up the backyard stove.

One Saturday, we finished early. The Postman asked me if I wanted to ride to Walmart with him and I told him sure. I hadn't been off The Road in a long time. I went home, solar-showered, and changed clothes.

He carried a big cooler in his big 4x4 Nissan pickup. I grabbed ice and some lamp oil. The kerosene I'd been using in the lamps was giving me headaches in this unbearable heat. I also bought puppy food and snack foods. Then he said he had to go to Tractor Supply – it was a dream place. It gave me ideas like reading a catalog. Boy, could I spend some money in there.

I had learned to think way ahead. We don't do that living in the cities because we're so close to any market or store we need.

I always used my Sundays for cleaning and cooking as much as I could eat. And I did eat. I was using a lot of energy at that job and I knew I had to maintain.

~ ~ ~

The two Mexicans and I were firing out wood. We had five- to six-foot stacks all the way around the barn. The wrapper, who only came now every two or three days to wrap bundles, was loving it. He got used to our speed. It didn't profit him to drive all the way out for a few hours.

We had piles of wood all over the place. They would move the wrapping tables all over. They used the fork lift because the tables were very heavy. It was very hard to get around and you had to be very careful. We threw the wood into our piles without looking. If you crossed into our paths, so be it. You got dinged on whatever part of your body happened to get in the way.

My birthday came and went. I was so relieved because I knew it would soon begin to get cooler. And it did, in the form of a raging twelve-inch rain. Great! I had already figured out the mud and wasn't driving in it or crossing those bridges which floated off their moorings at any given moment. I had a lot of catching up to do on my place.

It rained for days. The woodpile lot was muddy and slopped up into a nasty mess. At first, The Postman came and got me because the roads at that end were underwater. Then the bridges floated. The Mexicans could get in the back way, but I wasn't driving twenty extra miles to make The Ego happy.

The pups and I were happy and I ate cold canned soup and canned stew. And sweet rolls.

I decided that as soon as production stopped I would look for a stove. I had to do something different. I had cooked outside all last winter and it worked on cold, miserable days as well as on hot miserable days, but I wanted to be able to cook on rainy days, too, in my Someday Kitchen.

My cistern was running over. I hated losing that water, I but had no way to save it.

My sons came back from Missouri. Their job ended and they swung by to visit. The Oldest fell in love with Charlie Brown, the collie pup, who was now a raging adolescent. Thank God I didn't have any electric cords for him to chew up.

Charlie Brown relaxing in the living room. The plastic in the background hides the original summer kitchen where the Chinaberry tree crushed the roof.

A couple of years later, he would take Charlie Brown when he moved to Minnesota for a line job. Charlie Brown lived to be a very old dog. He was a beautiful, loving, smart dog and, sadly, had to be put down in 2011 because he had a form of cancer.

Dog was very different than Charlie Brown. He was a big silent dog. He didn't bark much but when he was older, became a sneaky attacker. If you weren't careful when you got out of your car or truck, he would be on you and you were dog bit.

By December 15, production had about shut down until next April. The businesses that bought our pallets of wood had all they would be able to sell for the season. Many of them wrote their contracts that way. If they needed a few pallets, they would come get me. The Mexicans would leave in December and return home, but they would be back in the spring. It was a sad time for me as I'd become used to the companionship.

~ ~ ~

I had almost hated my first winter. It was all new and I had nearly frozen. But this second winter, I was acclimated to the ole house and had a handle on good chunks of wood for the wood burner. There was always end butt waste from the logs and I had hauled loads of them home. Some fit right in the burner but others need splitting. I tried to pop them, but all they did was dig down in the dirt or flip over. Dangerous when you're swinging an axe. I thought for a bit and knew what would help. I went back to the dump and dug out an old brake drum. It worked perfectly. I would prop the butts on it and aim for the middle of the butt to split it. It took a while for me and the axe to get the hang of it, but once I did, I went to town on them. Soon, I had piles of short pieces, enough to bank the burner so I didn't need to restart it every day.

I loved that axe. It was perfectly balanced. People would see me outside splitting and would look at me like I must be nuts. Those were our weekend warriors, the city folk who had places along The Road for weekends and vacations. Lord help us.

At one time I was known as Axe Annie. It was a fun time. The physical exercise was so good for me. My muscles had toughened up, and I had more lung power. I was tougher all-around, both physically and mentally, and I felt a sense of freedom I'd never before known.

I tried to get as many loads of the butts as I could. Otherwise, The Ego would push them up in piles and spend the winter burning them. What a dummy, burning up good wood. One time I went down for my loads and Fake Fanny came out and told me I owed her $10.00 a load. What?? I guess she was smarter than The Ego, but I told her I didn't think so. Before things got nasty, though, the old Postman came out and told her – a reminder I would hear many times – this was his place and I could take whatever wood I wanted or needed.

It wasn't long before I was well-set for the winter. I pretty much had the wood separated with the driest on one side and the greenies on the other, all covered by (ugh, yuck) blue tarps. I called it critter housing. Spiders, snakes, and scorpions loved the shelter. I would have to thump each stick of wood to dislodge the creepy crawlers. They could get in the house by themselves. I wasn't giving them a free ride.

Isn't life strange?

I sat first chair for 4 years in music and had years of ballet lessons. I was a top seller for GM in 1979 and 1980. I worked in dry cleaning for years, raised my kids, and studied for a degree in mental health.

All were nice, clean, dignified jobs in a nice, clean, dignified world. And now here I was, doing something so opposite to all that yet, unbelievably, it made me so happy. I loved to scout the woods, looking for and identifying critter signs. I fished for my supper and saved water in a hole in the ground. I had no finger nails, and my shins would take years to clear up from all the dings from wood-knots. My hair was getting long. It was sun-bleached and so shiny from the rain water. And I went to sleep at night to the sounds of nature. It was peaceful and at last, I was at peace.

If you ever find peace, hang on to it. Don't let it go. Follow your dreams. Fight it through.

~ ~ ~

I loved to sit on the front porch on Sunday to read and drink my black spiced tea, a new discovery. All of a sudden, The Ego and Fake Fanny showed up. They told me to hurry, that they wanted to catch some new-born orphaned pigs. The real truth was they wanted me to catch them.

I don't know why The Fanny was terrified of them. She screamed like a banshee when we wanted to put them in the extended cab. So we swung by the house and got a king size pillow case and a long swimming pool dip net.

Let me say here – *never* underestimate new-born piglets. They ran like Arabian studs. We must have chased them for five miles through brush, up and down roads. If these babies hadn't been newborns and half starved to death, we would have never caught them. We – (As in me. The Fanny stayed in the truck and The Ego was so out of shape from dope and booze) – chased them into a thicket, dip netted the last two of the five, put them in the pillow case, tied the thing up, and put them in the bed of the truck. Then we had to run to the feed store to get some sour mash for them. We sold two at the feed store, they took one, and I took two. Selling the two paid for the feed, but now what would I do with two new-born piglets?

It would be hilarious.

Charlie Brown had grown. He was about the height of a mama pig. His coloring was golden orange and white with some brown. Those two babies took to him immediately. They nuzzled and tried to nurse from him. Yes, I had them in the house, and remember Charlie B was a male dog. Piggies trying to nurse on him was the funniest thing I ever saw. He would jump and howl and turn and look at them. Like I said, hilarious!

I had hot water, so I made them some mash with canned milk and they ate like they were on their last meal. Then, suddenly, they dropped down and went to sleep with the dogs and slept all night. They kept trying to nuzzle Charlie Brown all night, too, until he finally jumped on bed with me to avoid the two nursing babies. And for the next few weeks they would chase Charlie Brown relentlessly, trying to nurse on the poor boy.

Hilarious!

Charlie Brown relaxing on a piece of carpet next to the $18 wood burner.

~ ~ ~

We were coming into the last of winter. On trips when I ventured into town with the hateful ole truck, I'd run into yard sales. I found lots of old blankets, carpet squares, and a few things to add a homey touch to the ole house.

One day, the old, worn-out truck quit on me in an intersection and I had it hauled across the scales and sold for scrap. By word of mouth, I found an old red and white, three-quarter ton, five-speed pickup. I got a great deal on her. She was an absolute mud hog when she was loaded with seven- to eight-hundred pounds of split wood in the back for weight. There were times when that old truck and The Postman's would be the only ones moving in the woodpile because of the mud.

One night, after working late, I discovered why I got her so cheap. The wiring harness was a lamp cord – yep, 110-volt lamp cord. It seems the harness had burnt up and the usual make-do attitude of country folk won out. She ran fine, though there was one problem – the wiring couldn't carry the headlights and tail lights. Many was the night I drove home in the dark praying I wouldn't run across the Black Bull. He was a common sight, standing around on the road at his leisure. It was funny to a point, but could have been deadly if I hit him.

My '64 Chevy 3/4 ton, 5-speed workhorse. Boy Dog is happy to pose with me but Samantha prefers to lounge in the shade.

The house was bare when I got there and I didn't have curtains. The windows were narrow and in the summer, I needed all the air I could get. The only windows that would ever be covered were the three north-facing windows. The winter wind blew right through them.

I had moved back to the small bedroom for winter. Changing bedrooms was a ritual I would have every winter and summer.

I put the carpet squares down around the wood burner for the pups and banked the stove. If I blocked the gap under the front door (that's the way she breathed), she would burn slow all night. It's strange how you discover the mechanics of things. In the morning I would pull my sand bag away from the door gap and the burner would take off.

My two baby pigs ate like pigs, but began to think like dogs. They were growing, so I blocked them in the kitchen while I worked. They were their own wrecking crew. I put down paper for them and they house-broke themselves. The pups were house-broke and all was well. Tippy hunted, treed squirrels, chased rabbits, and kept an eye on the babies, but would stand back from the piglets, which I found funny.

The last part of March, I got another puppy that would become my protector for seventeen years. She was one of a litter of seven. As I got to work one morning, I heard shots. The Postman came out and told me The Ego was killing the puppies with a 30.06. Brave guy, huh? More like a gutless wonder. He didn't know what he was going to do with his son. Hell, I didn't know either but I asked how many were left. He told me one and that it was hiding under a pile of wood, terrified.

I ran to The Ego's backyard and came close to throwing up when I saw the carnage. The only reason I didn't was that I was totally livid!

"Don't kill it," I screamed at him. "I'll take it."

I discovered it was a female. She was about six weeks old. I had to move lots of old lumber to get to her. My God, the little thing was shivering and tried to bite me with her baby teeth but I got her, put her under my jacket, and took her to my truck. I opened my Vienna sausages and fed her, then wrapped her up in my jacket and finally, she began to stop shivering. It would be a long time before I cooled down past murdering the drunk idiot. I worked all day, taking my breaks to hold my little terrified bundle. I would call her Samantha or Sammy. And Woo-woo because when she got older and I talked to her, she would make a woo-woo sound.

Sammy Woo-woo would become a fierce protector. She was a short fat girl and never growled. She just went for the parts she could bite. I became her baby. She would circle me, keeping the dogs away from me. She knew no fear, and only backed up for Tippy. The ole girl stayed with me for many years, until, two years after losing Tippy, I had to have her put down because by then, she was old and blind and could only follow me by smell.

The day Sammy came into my life was the day I realized the cruelty of dope and booze. Watching The terrible Ego, I could see the waste, and came to understand how miserable a human could be.

~ ~ ~

I now had four dogs, two pigs, and would soon have a new housemate.

Spring production took off and I welcomed the coming time change. I needed more daylight hours. It took everything I had to work and care for me and my brood.

The Ego brought two of his friends to work for him and to live in an ole house that I didn't know existed on the back of the property. Of course, they were drunks. It got interesting.

My daughter was in Germany with my son-in-law, who was in the Army. I had called the boys. They were coming the following Sunday to build me that outhouse.

I had a list of stuff I asked them to bring. Except for work, groceries, or trips to the feed/hardware store, I rarely left the place.

~ ~ ~

The boys showed up the following Sunday with plywood, 2x4s, and tin. Then it dawned on them – oops how do we cut this wood? Well I sure wasn't jumping off the porch on it. My hamstring still gave me trouble.

I suggested we go to The Postman's and off we went. I left them and a cooler full of beer with him. About three hours later – the old Postman was a talker and a longneck drinker – they came back and pulled the completed outhouse out of the truck, shiny new tin roof and all.

They figured out where to put it, well away from my cistern, and dug a hole for it. They were working hard, so I cooked them some bacon and eggs and skillet toast. And I had the animals out for exercise. Of course, the piglets were still chasing Charlie Brown, still thinking he was their momma. The boys got the biggest kick out of it, even if CB didn't.

They went back to work and finally they called me to see their handy-work. Of course I properly oooo'd and ahhh'd. Then I opened the door and for a few moments, I couldn't figure out what was wrong with it. Then it hit me and I went into hysterical laughter. I laughed 'till tears ran down my face as they looked at me like I had lost my mind, probably thinking geez, it was just an outhouse! It was an outhouse, alright, but there was no "out." They had forgotten to make holes in the proper places. When I finally quit laughing, they were

73

loading her up to go back to The Postman's to cut out some proper holes in it.

The outhouse always had scorpions, spiders, and possums!

Even as grown men, my three boys were so close that when they had the chance to get together, they were so happy with each other that it didn't matter what was going on. The hole-less outhouse became one more memory for me to store in the happy list.

I would tease them about it for a long time. I loved those guys and they loved me. They were my three, blued-eyed musketeers.

~ ~ ~

The next week began with a sneaky cold front and a visit from The Boy and his horse. He came flying up as fast as he could ride, calling me. He had found a new-born fawn on the road, curled up and cold. He tied his horse off and we went back down the road.

The baby was still there. I could see blood trailing into the woods. Poachers. Someone had shot the doe in the night. It was a wonder someone hadn't run over the little buck.

The fawn was still wet and sticky. The coating was his protection, some kind of odor barrier to keep him invisible to predators.

I didn't have a bottle, so I headed to The Postman's house. He had all kinds of little critter stuff. He told me he was going to town and would get me some calf manna.

Lord, that fawn was beautiful. I had to report I had him...or did I? Fish and Wildlife kept a close watch on the quantity of bucks in the area. I didn't want them to decide to kill him or even take him, so I made the decision to keep my mouth shut. I called him Knight Rider.

~ ~ ~

The boys had used the scraps of plywood and woodpecker wire to build me an outside piglet pen. It was great. I could feed them and leave them outside and there'd be no more chasing them. I had to come home at break times to feed Knight Rider and I put the piglets out then.

All the little ones grew so quickly. Knight Rider's nursery was my Someday Kitchen. He would get up and come to me when I came into the house. The floor had an old linoleum covering and it turned out he was a paper-training kind of guy too.

He was displaying his wild, natural habits. He would snort and put his head down and paw at the floor with his tiny hooves. When I would return home, I'd find him lying curled up and quiet, waiting for me to feed him. He would stand on those gangly legs and make a squeaking sound and come to me with a kinda jumping walk.

Putting the piglets outside later in the day helped with predators. Coyotes would have gotten them at night. Charlie brown was real happy about that. He was growing and although Dog was much younger, the Rottweiler in him made him seem older. He was a big dog.

The day we found Knight Rider, The Postman came by to see about him. He tried to tell me what I already knew, that someday Knight Rider would have horns, and that despite my kindness, he would always remain a buck and be dangerous. I knew that and wanted to give him a chance to grow and become a big buck. Tippy continued to be okay with just a slight tremor once in a while.

The piglets kept on following Charlie Brown when I let them out of the pen at night. They didn't try to run off. I guess my place had become Home Sweet Home to them. Sammy was a silent puppy. She wasn't doing as well I thought she should, so at night, I began to take her to bed with me. She curled up in a ball and stayed close to me.

It was a three-ring circus at night, with me so tired, everybody wanting to eat, and having to fire up the outside kitchen. At night, in the winter, it was rough, but more daylight was on its way. And I would soon find a stove – a monster really – and my Someday Kitchen would begin to take shape.

~ ~ ~

The Postman came by to see if I wanted to go to the store. Yes! I was running on empty and needed some things. We ran into Huntsville and on the way back, he stopped at a small convenience store. The old folks who owned it sold his kind of beer, the Long Necks he couldn't always get at Walmart. We pulled up to the store and there was my stove!

The old folks had remodeled their kitchen and gone totally electric. Just the day before they had set that stove out front. It was an old propane model and was just what I needed. I was almost afraid to ask how much they wanted for it and was flabbergasted when they said $25.00. I dug out my money and paid them on the spot.

They warned me that it was heavy.

"Not a problem," I said.

"No," they said, "it's *really* heavy."

Being respectful, I told them I'd get some help and be back. Help? I needed all the hands I could get. They were not exaggerating when they said it was really heavy. That stove was the heaviest thing I had ever tried to pick up. And getting it in the house through the small doors would take a huge effort. It was an old double-oven with four burners and a huge griddle in the middle that was perfect for making skillet toast and pancakes.

It would be the weekend before I could get the boys back out. It was a long ways for them and they always had stuff to do. But I would soon have an indoor kitchen, or the beginnings of one, and begin to recover from some of the harshness of the life I'd been leading.

Little did I know the fittings to my propane tank and the bottom of the stove would cost a bundle. Murphy's Law always prevails.

~ ~ ~

I was at work when the boys showed up on Saturday. They came down to the woodpile and The Postman said he'd take them to get the stove. I told them I would be home in a bit.

When they got to the house with the stove, they had backed their truck up to the back door and scared Knight Rider so bad he had jumped the barrier and was hiding in the bedroom. Geez. In my excitement I had forgotten about him. They spent time holding him and marveled at his beauty. Eventually, he settled down, but I still got the same warning from them I got from The Postman.

"Mama, you do know this is a buck, don't you?"

Geez.

The next few hours were something else. My boys are very strong. Still, they grunted and sweated and cussed and gave me *that look* – the "what did you get us into here" look.

They had to make a trip to the hardware/feed store to buy connections but by dark, the door was back on and I had the beginning of my Someday Kitchen. It would be the mainstay of my life as production got bigger and bigger in the woodpile.

To this day I believe that ole stove saved my life. Until you live out in the elements, you don't know what a toll it takes on your health.

~ ~ ~

Ok I was human again. I had spent over a year cooking in the yard. And now, here I was with my new indoor stove. My beautiful new friend had been well cared for and was in such good shape. I heated some water to clean her. Pancakes and a chocolate skillet cake were my first meals and I had coffee ready in such a short time in the mornings, I found that when I woke, I could sit and for the first time, actually smile to begin my day.

The old oven worked beautifully and I baked ahead for the week. There never was a loaf of bread, then or now, that tasted as good as my first loaf in her. And a 25-gallon tank of propane lasted forever.

My coffee making went faster, though I still used the camp pot, and I could have some toast and eggs before I went to work.

My cooler was my fridge. In the summer, it was a test to keep it cold, but using the freezer at The Postman's for keeping ice helped. If I bought ice in town, it was usually half-melted by the time I got home.

I would rethink buying meat now. I was meat hungry. I made some meat loaf, fried up chickens, and packed it cold for work meals, which really helped.

My baby critters kept growing. I would let them out to roam and play. The little buck would lick the dirt. He had to have the minerals to survive. Sometimes he chewed tree bark. I bought a mineral block and set it down for him to lick, but all the animals would use it. Cool! The baby pigs were becoming monsters, little garbage guts that ate anything. And I had to start keeping the male dogs separate at feeding times because Dog and Charlie would fight.

~ ~ ~

My work was picking up now and I would soon be introduced to a three-ring circus.

This year would be the hardest with hiring new people. Most didn't last. And I received word my VA short term widow's pension would be approved.

Yes! Yes!! Now I could do a bit more for my comfort. And I would have a little leverage with the Fake Fanny. She couldn't bully me now that I had a hand of cards.

I could stock up on lamp oil, which wasn't bad in the summer with the long daylight hours. And I needed some shoes.

I also received notice Jim's headstone had been set at Ft. Sam Houston National Cemetery. It was a hard letter to read. I couldn't be there to see it, but at last he had it.

~ ~ ~

The Ego's buddy, The Bully, showed up again, dragging his wife and two old school friends who were just as big drunks and dopers as he was.

One was a master Mechanic. There wasn't a thing mechanical he couldn't fix. The other one was a Sad, little Guy. He mostly stayed drunk and was the butt of a lot of harsh words.

The Ego decided that The Mechanic would be the yard boss. Yeah right. The three Mexicans came back and they had some friends who wanted to work. We paid little attention to the new yard boss. All he wanted to do was ride on the fork lift all day. He was supposed to be wrapping, but that didn't happen.

He immediately started fussing at the Mexicans and I told him he needed to back off. We'd been sitting in the woodpile for two seasons and did just fine before he showed up. The Mexicans and I took care of our splitters. We changed the oil every Friday, gassed them up, and moved them so we could clean out all the wood shavings and scraps.

The Mechanic would shut down production just to rake the barn. The Postman would hear us shut down and come out to see the problem. There would be many fights over The Bully and The Sad Guy – and the Bully's wife. Boy did she think she was special. They wanted me to teach her how to run a splitter. Ha! Not in this lifetime.

The Mechanic and his girlfriend, The Bully and his wife, and The Sad Guy would all move into the old house on the back of the property. That would turn out to be a drunken, dope-smoking, fighting mess.

They never got to work at first light and The Postman was so angry. He paid all the bills and they were spending all their money on their habits. And a war would start when they assigned The Bully's wife to pile my log butts up for me.

The Bully was supposed to go on the truck to help unload pallets. What they wound up doing was drinking in the truck and then they'd come home in foul moods and take it out on us.

The Bully's wife spent all her time flirting with the Mexicans. They tried their best to ignore her. I had to yell over the splitters at her to load me. She was a real pain, all dressed up and prancing around. It made her mad to think she had to work for her money because she was so special. Yeah, right.

She started throwing log butts in my pile. I told her to be careful not to hit me and that's exactly what she did. She threw a big oak butt and whacked me on the shin. Boy did it ever hurt.

When I came up off the splitter, she was in a dead run. She had done it on purpose, the spoiled brat. I threw a butt and hit her and she started hollering. The Postman came out and asked what the "H" was going on, so I told him.

I filled him in on her silly prancing around. He said, "Oh, she is going to be a problem."

Yep and we would see the problem often. I had to remind The Postman that me and the Mexicans had been out here in all the bad weather for months and hadn't had any problems working. He agreed. The Mexican hands had been respectful, hard working men and we all got along great. We weren't there to be anybody's whipping post or to feed their grandiose egos. We knew our jobs and worked hard.

I knew would have to deal with The Bully soon, but oak butts worked wonders as an equalizer.

~ ~ ~

When the truck got in that night, we didn't pay any attention. In a little bit, I saw The Bully coming back down the hill. He came in the yard and headed straight for me. Okay, party time.

He reached down and shut off my machine and boy did that make me mad. I asked him what he thought he was doing. Shutting down someone's machine is a dangerous thing to do if you didn't know where their hands were.

And I got the, "Did you hit my wife?"

"Yep. She hit me" And I let him know right up front she had deliberately whacked me.

I pulled up my sweat pants leg and showed him the ugly bruise and torn flesh. He started to get closer and I reached down and grabbed me a nice heavy oak butt and asked him if he'd like to feel how it hurt and he stopped dead in his tracks. He never bothered me again, but she would try. He had sense enough to back off and let me work. She didn't have any sense at all.

By now there were seven Mexicans and myself. One was a tall, greying gentleman about my age. He would later present a quandary I never before faced.

~ ~ ~

Business began to pick up. The Fake Fanny had the nerve to ask me if I could go a week without a payday.

Nope!

"Well you're getting your pension now," she said. The Postman must have said something to them.

I turned and went to The Postman and told him, "Look, I work doing a man's job. I have always done the very best job I could, considering the bad conditions."

He told me that they had that argument. The reason was, they wanted to go to Nascar Races and needed the money. What was wrong with these people?

I got paid.

The next week, I would find out they were paying The Drunk and The Bully more than the Mexicans and me. Around we went again. And I told The Postman I needed more money. I was working twelve to fourteen hours a day and it just wasn't right. I had the great challenge of seeing that people got to work and that we had the needed number of pallets done at the end of the day. I got my money.

Why were we being treated so badly? Dope. It does that to people. But it would take a turn for the better next week.

The Mexicans and I worked from about 5:30 in the morning till dark six to seven days a week now, firing out wood, and getting the new guys trained. One of them could run the forklift and was a good chainsaw hand, but we only had him that one season. He was a skilled hand and found a job with a rancher that included living quarters. We sure hated losing him. He was very good at his job.

As for the bunch in the house in the woods, they didn't show up 'till late in the morning. We had so much to do and they would come in and stop production wanting to know how much we had done. Stupid jerks. All you had to do was look at the mounds of split wood. We were averaging about 16 to18 pallets a day now and the new hands would speed things up. I don't think anyone knew how hard those people worked. And they never refused my request to do something.

The poor Sad Guy showed up half in the bag and walked into the forklift. I heard the screaming. As the forklift turned to bring a load, he walked into the forks and it smashed his thumb so bad it had to be amputated at the big knuckle. The Mechanic was on the forklift, and he hadn't been sober in years. He didn't even hear us yelling at him.

The Postman rushed him to the hospital. Sad Guy was in shock. When The Postman got back, I shut down and went to the house with him. They kept Sad Guy overnight. He was already in poor physical shape.

I told him we couldn't keep this up, that these people were endangering everybody, and it was nerve wracking. I also told him The Bully was a nasty little man and that he was pushing the Mexicans too far.

When The Ego, The Bully, and the Fake Fanny got home from delivering, The Postman told The Ego his buddies had to go. Period.

81

All the cussing and jaw-fighting made us all nervous. Two of the Mexicans could speak English, so they could sense it wasn't good.

The Mechanic had connections with drug dealers and The Ego and The Bully were fighting them having to leave. The Postman told them they could stay in the house until they found someplace else to live, but to stay out of the woodpile.

I knew The Postman didn't need all this aggravation. He worried about me and the crew and I worried about him and the idiots.

The next day, The Postman came out to tell me they had a new convenience store contract. Cool! But we would have to have 24 pallets on the ground every night. I told him we needed more hands and more splitters and not 25-tonners. We needed more power. The big ones could take the hours and the splitting went faster. We got two new 35-tonners the next week.

And the next week, I would be made yard boss. It wasn't a position of power, just more work, but I didn't mind. At the time I had tunnel vision and was focused on my job and my little nursery.

~ ~ ~

We were short of wood and had two days off. No problem. I had plenty to do at the house.

All the critters were outside. The pigs had learned to jump their fence and followed the dogs around. Knight Rider tolerated them, but stayed to himself, grazing and licking the dirt and the mineral block. He was still bottle-fed, but his fawn spots were gone. How strange it was to see wild creatures commingle with domestics.

The Mexicans came to my place to buy one of the pigs. It was sad for me, but I needed to thin my heard. The one left alone stuck to Charley Brown. In fact, it followed the dogs, ate dog food, and in the following weeks, slept outside with them.

I kept Tippy and Sammy in the house. The males were beginning to be watch dogs and didn't leave the porch at night. Sammy was a quiet girl. I think the terror of that day she was abandoned kind of changed her. She didn't like anybody but me and would hide if anyone came around.

Knight Rider was about five months old. He still took two bottles a day, but wandered farther and farther and I wouldn't stop him. Nature was calling him and that's where he belonged. He was a beautiful buck and practiced butting the dogs.

Samantha relaxing.
I was her 'baby.'

I didn't practice with my shot-gun because I didn't want Knight Rider to get use to the sound. I wanted him to run if that time ever came. And it would, long before I wanted it to.

For now, I could only hope the pack of coyotes didn't get him, but at night, he slept near the dogs, like he knew they were protection.

I swept the ole house. I left it open all day, but The Road was so dusty, it all blew in through the front door and window. But it was beginning to look homey.

I had known I couldn't keep up the pace in the woodpile and cook outside because it took so long and if you're out in the boonies, off-grid, and by yourself, time could be your enemy. Now, my Someday Kitchen had the old railroad cabinet, my old enamel table, and my life-saving stove.

Winters were long and at times, wet and windy. Summers were hotter than jalapeños and could be murderously lethal, but I had a grip on it all. I could keep groceries, critter food, and all my books coming. All was well.

I would go into 1998 doing what I had always wanted to do. I was my own person. I wasn't arrogant, or prideful. I was self-assured, knowing, and at long last, truly at peace.

~ ~ ~

The next day was a Sunday. I was splitting log butts for my wood burner when I heard the tractor. It sounded big and it stopped at my gate. I went out, and there was the reclusive neighbor again, the one who had been in the black Ford Dually who had helped me get un-lost when I first moved here. He was back to mow the meadow and around the back of the house. We shook hands and I opened the gate and in he came with his monster brush hog. Now and again, he would bring the big tractor and keep the Bahia grass down. It was a tough grass. The cows had loved it, but now that they were gone it quickly took over the meadow.

I made fresh coffee.

The Ford man had many acres and raised Black Angus. He also had a regular job and drove long distances to work. Every day when he got home he would change clothes and check his herd. They were all tagged. If he happened to come by when the boys were visiting, he would stop and talk to them. I didn't know he was giving them updates on me.

Why did everyone think I needed taking care of? During the big Y2K scare, he stopped by one day and told me, "You're the only one out here that won't be affected."

Well, I didn't know what a Y2K was, but when I started reading about it in my *Backwoods Home Magazine*, I knew he was right.

I was stronger, my mind was in a great place, and the ole house was looking homey. Work was hard – terribly demanding – but I was holding on to my money. I had a hidey hole.

The Boy on the horse was nearing graduation. He brought me an invitation to it. Of course I would go. He was at that half-man half-boy stage, so polite and so gangly. He was going to sell his two horses for a truck. I told him to quit being in such a hurry, to enjoy being free for now.

What I didn't tell him was that the world out there would eat him alive if he let it.

~ ~ ~

By the time I got to the woodpile Monday morning, it was cool and would soon be sunny. We marveled over the two new splitters. I still ran the 40-tonner. We wanted to be outside in the sunshine. Being cooped up in that three-sided barn breathing the fumes wore on us.

To move the splitters, we used The Postman's 4-wheeler. It had a trailer hitch. By laying the hydraulic cylinders down, they were easy to move. Of course, we knew to let the hydraulic fluid run back down before we restarted them.

One of the new Mexicans tried his hand at wrapping. Once he got the hang of it, that left five of us splitting. It also left our forklift/chainsaw man free to do his thing. He was very good with the chainsaw, very safe. He always looked around before he started it.

We went through so many chains cutting the butts because there was no way to keep them out of the dirt. Then The Postman found an electric chain sharpener and boy did it save a bundle. The chainsaw man learned to run it, too. He had better eyes than The Postman. He was a very good man as were the two originals. They were all hard-working, diligent men.

Of all the tiny pieces of equipment, the ones we cherished were the hatchets. Sometimes, you had strings of wood that wouldn't cut or that the splitter missed. There's nothing like having your piece of wood be hooked up to another piece when you went to throw it on the pile. It would whack ya – on the shin, of course.

I don't know why, but I loved the rhythm of the splitters – load, split in half, split the halves into quarters, then toss on the pile. I became the fastest at it, maybe because I really did enjoy it. I guess it was just one of those things, and with the rhythm, I didn't think about my grief or my problems or what would happen to me.

The newly cut log butts would be anywhere from twelve inches to three feet across, and heavy. Some were even bigger. They were rolled or thrown on our side piles. To remained seated and roll those big guys in front of you under the wedge was back-breaking, but muscle building. Many times, when I got a butt under my wedge, I'd have to kick it back against the housing.

I would breathe in the scent of the fresh-popped wood. Red oak has a beautiful smell, but the ultimate was hickory, which has a cinnamon smell. It was the best.

There was a lot of what I call wood scrabbles – slivers of wood.

One day, I had an idea. I found a box and a rake and started gathering them. I took them home and put some in coffee cans, poured in kerosene to cover them, then put the lid back on and set them outside, one for my water tubs and one for the burner. They became my fire-starters, replacing the pine cones, and saved a lot of problems lighting my fires.

One day, The Postman came out and got me. He wanted me to be yard boss. He told me he had borrowed on his house to start this business and it was his backside at stake. He said I would answer only to him and that I wasn't to let Fake Fanny boss me. He needed someone to get the job done and The Ego wasn't getting it done.

The Ego was a very smart man, he had all kinds of ideas, but he didn't have the means within himself to get them done. He was a truck punisher. He pushed equipment to the max. He'd get the loads delivered, but be *in the bag* before he got home, which was another reason he didn't get things done.

I had an idea about only scheduling delivery loads on certain days. On the in-between days, we could haul timber and split wood. That way, we could always have the needed pallets and be way ahead. It would be a lot less stress on everybody. Besides, many of the contracts only accepted loads on certain days anyway. Plan, and then follow through.

When loggers were out cutting pines, The Postman would buy the hardwoods on the land. But he needed to get them to us. He had an old Ford with a 10-speed Road Ranger and a float. The Ego would take the forklift (and The Bully and his ole lady, too) and make a day of it.

Then they found an old horizontal splitter. Oh, man, that was not for me. That would be way too much lifting. They hired a big fat guy. Oh, was he a griper. He tried to change everything we were doing. He was put on the horizontal, thankfully, away from us. He lasted a week.

My men were happy campers. We were fired up every morning, slinging log-butts, and watching the pallets accumulate.

We began to look like a real business. I was so proud of the guys. The Postman asked me if I thought the men resented me being the yard boss. I told him, nawww. I treated them with great respect and gained their respect. I didn't wimp out, and I didn't ask them to do any more than I did.

~ ~ ~

I was getting a ton of mail from lawyers. The Postman would bring my mail down to the yard if he had to run for gas.

I had to get so many letters notarized that I made friends with the ladies at the bank. I would run to the bank with my cap on and gloves in hand. It was funny. I was all dirty, but healthy, tanned and happy.

And speaking of gloves, I found a kind I really liked. The longer I wore them, the softer they got. I still have my last pair behind the seat of my truck. They're so well-used the tag's worn off.

One morning this week would bring some bad news for The Postman.

~ ~ ~

When The Postman's' wife died, he put his daughter-in-law on his checking account. There was a lot of paperwork and insurance to settle and he had a lot of property and equipment.

He met me at the barn when I got there and told me Fake Fanny had drained the business checking account and taken off like a scalded dog. She was a pill-popper, had a monster ego, and was fake down to her toes. He was going to be gone all day, changing all the accounts, and trying to borrow money to pay the men and keep going.

The Ego sat in front of the TV and pouted and drank. It would be a harsh week. We stayed out of the way.

Then The Bully's wife started her mess. The Bully had to take the truck and deliver. While he was out, she would be in and out of The Ego's house. I could see it coming and it would not be good.

The Postman stopped her one morning and told her she needed to go back to the ole house. She flounced past him to The Egos house, which sat behind The Postman's, as if he had no say as to what happened on his property. He was trying to get The Ego off his butt to get us some logs. We had orders to fill.

It was like a nightmare. We wanted to work, but it was null and void without any logs. The men drove all the way out every morning. It was 30 to 35 miles for them. They were good workers and I was afraid we'd lose them.

That week the men had to wait for their payday. It was late by the time The Postman came in. We quickly figured the men's wages. He had brought them some beer and tried his best to soothe the angry and irritated feelings of the men who needed their pay.

We had the weekend off, which was good. I was tired and the drama was wearing on me. As I sat on the old porch that Saturday morning, I reflected on what I thought would be different here in the backwoods. I had the naive notion that I had left meanness and strife from other humans behind me when I moved off the grid. I thought that I could cut it out of my life. But I couldn't, not completely. It's everywhere.

I would withdraw more, trying to ignore it all, but it was hard. We can't help but hear and feel things. People are people. Hard as it was, though, I would learn to tune them out and stay as far away from trouble-causing people as I could.

It was early and cool and the sun peeked out. I saw does in the meadows with their yearlings. Knight Rider saw them too. He would throw his head up snorting at the air and he'd scrape the ground. As I watched him, he edged closer to the herd. Three of the does turned to protect the yearlings and he knew it, too. But he didn't know what to do.

As the does moved off he started to follow them, but turned back. It wouldn't be long 'till he would follow them and not come back.

~ ~ ~

The critters in my nursery were growing up. My little piggy was a big girl. All summer she followed the dogs around. It was a funny sight, with Tippy leading Charlie Brown, then Dog and the Hog. Off they'd go. She would grunt as her little feet were doing double-time, trying to keep up with the dogs long-legged pace. It would be a long time before Sammy Woo-woo would follow Tippy.

In the summer heat, Charlie Brown and Dog would sleep under the front of the house and the pig would join them. But there came a time when she grew big enough that she couldn't get under there with them and she would squeal and grunt trying to wedge herself under the house. I knew she would be gone before long. Nature would call her and I would truly miss her. Charley Brown wouldn't, though. She had dogged him since day one. My critters would be thinning out.

I stopped bottle feeding Knight Rider. He now fed himself, grazing around the house. I always had water down for the dogs and I had to make a decision about that – to cut out all comforts for the buck. The pond was in the back and I needed to let him learn how to find his own way.

I walked to the back with all of the critters following me. Knight Rider followed us and when we got to the pond, he blew and snorted. He could smell the other deer had been there.

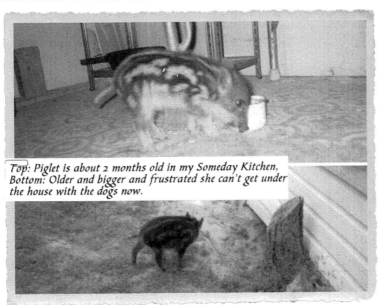

Top: Piglet is about 2 months old in my Someday Kitchen, Bottom: Older and bigger and frustrated she can't get under the house with the dogs now.

Suddenly, Samantha jumped in the pond and scared the bejeebers out of me. She bit at the water and swam and swam. She had found her place. She was a short but long baby girl. Roly-poly. And I laughed. Old Tippy just watched her. Then she started in the water, but backed up.

Sammy chased frogs and bugs for a while and then came out. I had found a way to reach her traumatized brain. Water therapy. I cried all the way back to the house. I had worried so much about this fuzzy bundle. She ran and jumped and barked at me and I thanked God. She would spend many hours at that pond, paddling slowly, biting at the water. If I couldn't find her near the house, I always knew where to look. Soon after, she discovered skunks.

That winter, I would watch the Knight Rider wander off. He came home off and on, but then I didn't see him anymore. I went to my little prayer place, a bit sad, but glad I was able to save his life. He would have another season. It would be a doe season so no bucks could be killed. And if he got past the poachers, he would have extra time.

I put the dogs out early one morning and walked all the way back to the very back side of the fifty. I walked the full fence perimeter and came upon the hog wallow, but it was deserted. Old boars would put you up a tree if you were lucky. If you weren't, they were swift and deadly. You had to shoot them dead in the head, between the eyes, to stop them, which is kind of hard to do while climbing a tree.

I didn't find my little buck. He had gone to find a herd. Life was a bit sad. My piggy baby would leave us, too, this coming winter.

Dog would leave the next summer with our young friend. He loved riding in The Boy's truck. They made a great pair and neither of them would be alone. And knowing Dog's disposition, he would protect my young friend.

After he left, the next time I would see The Boy, he would bring a wonderful surprise.

~ ~ ~

The Postman had to sell his small herd of mixed-breed cows to bail out the business. It was so traumatic for him. He kept one old girl, his original cow.

He cried as the truck came for his herd. I had to come off the splitter and get him in the house. He had nitro for his heart in a tiny bottle. I went out to the truck and got the papers and the count on the cows. The fellow who bought them said he was so sorry. He'd known the old Postman for years. I was really, really mad at those who caused this. The Postman sat in the house all day.

We had logs. The Ego had evidently gotten over his silly self and found a new place for logs. I would learn years later, he had stolen an out-of-state owner's timber.

I asked the Mexicans that day to take up my slack and I managed to get The Postman to bed. I stayed late, afraid he would have another heart attack. He asked me to call his Oldest Son and daughter. Whew! They said they would be right out. They lived about 200 miles away. It would be a long night.

The Ego and Fake Fanny would get a dose of my anger and the Oldest Son would stay for a week and help me. He took his dad to the doctor and he ran for gas and our ice and just in general helped us as much as he could.

The Postman had owned the place for 30 years and everything was on the line now, including his home and all his equipment, all for the love of his son, and for trying to help him get a grip on life.

I wanted to get a grip on him all right.

~ ~ ~

Winter was on us and we really had to sling some logs. Orders flowed in and we managed to get 48 pallets ahead.

I had to get to work on my ole house. I needed rolls of plastic to do the inside. The northeast wind blew right through the newest side of the house. Cold ain't the word for it.

Before the year was out, I would learn my Mother was in congestive heart failure. She would develop a rare, fast moving cancer and die ten days after my 59th birthday.

My sister-in-law had colon cancer. She would die a few weeks after my oldest brother, who would be killed at work – electrocuted by a hidden 220 volt wire. And then suddenly, a beloved brother-in-law would die of a heart attack at work. All four gone in a nine month period.

I reeled that year. My whole world filled with grief. Thank God our barbecue people needed wood. I would have lost my mind if I hadn't been able to keep busy.

Our hickory butts were twenty-four inches – full regular cords. The buyers brought their own low-boys, which were low-to-the-ground, pull-behind trailers. I split wood with a fury. I had to work it out, had to reconcile my brain to my helplessness.

The Postman always paid me separately – good money. I was the woodpile zombie.

~ ~ ~

I truly knew I belonged here, that it was my destiny. I was getting a grip on life again. It was so hard and I had to ask God why. A foolish question, I know now, but I think it's something we all ask during our lives.

I went to my little prayer area in the back and came upon the crippled doe with her new fawn. She didn't run. She just lay there with her baby, watching me as I prayed. Somehow, she knew I wasn't a threat. How astounding that was to me.

I liked the kind of peace I found out there when I would walk the back. One time, I found an old twisted pine tree and thought, that's how life is, twisted with emotions, trials, and tribulations.

But seeing the doe with her fawn was special. Somehow new life brings us back to sanity.

~ ~ ~

How I loved getting up in the mornings and making coffee in the camp pot on *my* stove as I made my eggs and toast.

Later, when we shut down for the rest of winter, I could make stews and chili. I even made fudge and kept on baking my own bread. I never since had an oven that baked like that one. The walls were thick, so they held heat better which made for a shorter, more even baking time. And peanut butter cookies – loved them!

The Bully was doing most of the deliveries now, leaving behind his pathetic, no-morals wife, much to our chagrin.

The Ego was bringing us timber. He was a marvel with all the heavy equipment. He fixed the old Caterpillar. I can't remember if it was a D9 Cat or what.

Many times he would use it to push huge trees down instead of hiring someone to cut it or sawing it himself. That was scary. Then he would drag them to the yard with The Postman's big French-built tractor. It was a regular-use tractor, a huge machine, but I can't remember the name of it.

We were really splitting now. We'd have races to see how many piles each of us could split. And at lunch, when the weather was cool, we'd have hatchet throwing contests. I always got beat. I would go home and practice, but the men had more height and muscle. But it was fun.

I had been told by a Green Beret to pick a weapon and become proficient with it. I had the .20 gauge shotgun, but what about other weapons. I know, I know, it's a guy thing, but I figured someday, a man might have to depend on a woman to back him up.

My grandson would graduate high school. I asked The Boy to come feed and water the animals for me. I was gone for two days. I couldn't believe the noise and the traffic in the city. I'd become like a barn-burnt horse – all I knew how to do was head home.

The Mexicans were all up in arms when I got back. The Tramp had decided she was boss. Oh good grief.

She didn't know I was back and when she came flouncing to the barn, I tied into her. I told her if I even heard of her getting close to this barn again, I would whip her worthless self. (I didn't use that kind of nice language. I used the kind of language she would understand.) She said she'd see about that and headed to The Ego's house. Whew! He came out cussing her, telling her to get her behind out of his way and off the yard. Just because she was having an affair with him while her hubby was delivering wood didn't mean she was making him any money. The Mexicans and I were.

Talk about a blow to her ego! I had to giggle. But when he got back, she would tell her hubby The Ego seduced her and they had a fist fight from hell. The Mexicans and I just stood back. The Bully and The Tramp moved the next day.

Now The Ego had to step up. We'd see. We went back to splitting.

That weekend I noticed lumber trucks running up and down the road. Oh, no! Another weekend warrior.

I planned a quiet weekend but needed to shop. I especially needed new socks. I changed socks frequently in the winter because my feet would get so wet and cold from the work it would take me an hour or so to get them warm at night.

On the way to town, I passed a garage sale and found a couple of chairs to go with my old table in the kitchen. I loved to sit there in the mornings and look at the meadow. At night I'd write or read, and the burners on the stove warmed up the little kitchen just great.

I started the truck and went to unlock the gate. A car stopped and two mangy-looking people, a woman and a man, got out. I started back to the truck. My pistol was on the seat. She pushed the gate open and just walked in. Whoa, I told her. You don't just come busting in here uninvited or before announcing yourself. I had two *No Trespassing* signs up.

She said, "Oh it's okay" and that she was building a house down so and so road.

"And?" I said. "And?"

"We'll be neighbors," she said. (Four miles down the road.)

Automatically my sixth sense had kicked in. The dogs kinda circled and growled.

It would turn out her mother had a piece of property, a beautiful little acre, and was building her a house way out here. Ok, why? I would later learn The Postman knew the family. This ole gal was a prescription drug addict as was her boyfriend, plus they were registered at the methadone clinic. I called them The Pill Heads.

Oh good grief, more trouble. I was beginning to think all of Houston was moving out here. The doper would try to zero in on The Postman 'cause she thought she knew him. She didn't, but who wanted to argue.

After reading a Tom Clancy book that weekend, I found my all-time saying – *Trouble Rides a Fast Horse*. Boy did it ever.

~ ~ ~

We went through the INS thing. All the Mexicans were legal, but someone had reported we were working illegals. I knew who it was, right as rain.

The Sad Guy finally recovered enough to come back out and work. He would stay with The Postman and help him run errands and help us load butts or clean up. It was good to see him come out of his cowed stance. He always came to me to make a list of things we needed and we got what we needed.

I had my tree up for Christmas. It was me and the four dogs.

Then my Youngest Son showed up with his buddy who owned an $80,000 RV, Geez!

They wanted to deer hunt and there were some old tree stands that had been there forever. But they didn't know I had been practicing my .20 gauge and there wasn't a deer within five miles of the place. But I wasn't telling them.

By morning they were pounding on the door. The heat wasn't working in the RV. I all but rolled on the floor laughing. I let them in, fired up the burner, and made them some links and scrambled eggs with skillet toast. They swore coffee never tasted better and said I'd made the best toast.

I was thinking, yeah, there you are in your refrigerated, heated, TV/VCR-playing, high-dollar toy with its heated showers and I'm building a fire for heat and feeding you. The whole thing was hilarious to me. And my ego kinda puffed up. I was maintaining a life while others camped out in comfort in the same environment.

~ ~ ~

We were just about through for the season. Only me and the 2 original workers remained. We cleaned up all the wood we had left and, once again, they would go home until we started up again next spring.

I would occasionally be called on to split private loads or if we needed a few pallets. I could average seven a day if I had the wood. One time, I split twelve pallets in a day, but that was a race against a machine called a Block Buster, a big, ugly breaking-down piece of junk.

It was dangerous to load. And it would throw chains off the saws. It was a deadly, horrible thing. And all the men would shake their heads no when asked if they would use it. We had our discussion about it and all agreed it wasn't safe. I was terrified of it.

The deal was, if I beat it, they would get rid of it. But that would come in the spring. In the meantime our new neighbors started with their daily crisis.

It was good to be home, to be able to cook stuff, to rest up, and to read and sign the lawyer's papers. That was never ending.

The new neighbors thought I was a mark. Too bad for them. They were a sneaky-acting pair and I never let them in my house.

Next thing I knew, they had The Postman running them to the store and to the methadone clinic. They said their car was broke down or out of gas or whatever. The truth was that they were too wasted to drive. They'd had many tickets and many wrecks and later, her Mother would call The Postman and tell him not to haul them anywhere. She sent a man out every week with groceries and to check on them.

The Postman began only taking them to the methadone clinic. His health wasn't very good and he had all he could do to keep up with the woodpile and all its problems.

Keeping the gate chained gave me an edge. As I sat in the house one cold, dreary day, I saw someone climb the gate. Me and the .20 gauge were out the door before he hit the ground. It was Pill Head's boyfriend. He wanted to know if I had any pain meds!!!

I brought the .20 up and told him, "You're gonna need more than painkillers if you don't climb back over that gate." He blustered up and I took a step back. I didn't want his death on me, but I didn't lower the gun. Back he went over the gate.

The next day, his girlfriend was down at the gate hollering at me. What did I mean pulling a gun on her boyfriend? I asked her, "Are you crazy you pilled-up b*****. This is my place. Don't ever come down here again, ever, and *never* cross my gate. Do you understand?"

She was so drugged up I wasn't sure she even understood what I was saying. So I said, "Here, let me show you what it sounds like." I turned and let off a round, then turned back to her and said, "That's the last thing you will ever hear. Got it?"

Oh my goodness did she whine to The Postman. He told them to stay away from me, that it was my place, and I had a right to protect myself.

The old Deputy Sheriff had made Constable and he would come by during the week every once in a while and shine his light on the house. I went into town, to the feed store, and asked the owner that if he saw him, to have him come out to see me.

I wasn't playing – period. I had fought for peace, for my life here, and I wasn't going to let this happen. I wouldn't be at the mercy of some drugged-out scum.

I was on alert. And I was glad it was winter and I was home, 'cause I figured they were looking for a soft robbery. They didn't know I didn't have much, but they weren't getting what I did have and they were not going to disturb my life. They had no brains left and that made them dangerous dopers in search of a fix.

~ ~ ~

Most days I would let the dogs out when I got up. That day was no different.

Tippy was the thinnest-coated of the dogs. It was strange she didn't seem to mind the cold as long as she could hunt. She took off, but it was nasty outside and Sammy Woo-woo came back in. The two boys had thick coats so the cold didn't bother them, but I kept them in and out of the wind at night. They didn't bother me. They were super in the house, mostly staying curled up by the burner.

It was really early in the morning and the two boys said nope. It was wet and cold out there and they weren't staying out. But Tippy wasn't with them.

I had heard the shots, light ones, like a .22 and thought it was probably squirrel hunters.

I called and called for Tippy but she didn't come back. I thought maybe she was after a squirrel or a mole. That was her latest thing, digging up moles or rats.

I knew she would often cross the road, so I put on my coat, got the .20 guage, and headed out across the road. It had been about an hour since I let them out. As I crossed the property, I kept looking, watching for hunters. I had walked about a half hour or so when I saw her. She was down. I ran like I was on fire.

She had been shot.

Tearing off my jacket, I wrapped her up and started to the house. I walked as gently as I could. It seemed to take forever. As I walked, it hit me. She had been pointed home. She'd tried.

I finally got home, put her in the truck, grabbed my keys, and tore off to The Vet's. I still had the gun and didn't even think about it until I was on the highway, driving like the devil was after me.

I knew where The Vet was on the highway, but I don't remember getting out of the truck. The nurse saw all the blood on my jacket and told me to follow her. She asked me what happened as they took my baby girl from me. I told her she was shot, a small caliber from what I heard, and she had been. The bullet had lodged at her kidney and he began to shave the area. Then they gave her sleepy time medicine and the nurse took me out.

She said, "You don't want to see this."

She had no idea what I had already seen in my life. It would have been almost comical if it hadn't been so dam serious.

I really don't know how long it was, but it seemed like hours before the doctor came out. I thanked God he was smiling, 'cause I wasn't. He said it was a .22 caliber. A tiny fraction more and it would have severed the artery feeding blood to her kidney and she wouldn't have made it.

He needed to keep her for a couple of days. I asked him to put my jacket in with her so she would smell me and not be afraid. I didn't want to leave her by herself but he reassured me that he stayed when he had very sick animals. They were never left alone.

I went in to stay with her for a while. She was hooked up to some fluids, just like people would be. I didn't have a clue what they were. I had to fill out paperwork. I didn't have a phone and didn't have a close neighbor. I could tell he thought me a bit strange. Oh well. I guess I was.

When I started home, I went to The Postman and told him what happened. He called the man who owned the property and asked who had been hunting on his place. The man told him no one, period. You just didn't hunt where cattle were kept. He was on his way.

I went home. I had to get money from my hidey hole. That took stealth with the new neighbors sneaking around. The last thing I needed was for them to see me. If they did, the money would soon be gone.

By that time, the owner of the property across the road showed up. He had seen Tippy hunting before and had gotten a kick out of the old, ragged dog. He was on horseback and would ride the place to see if he could find anyone. The Sheriff was on his way, too. It's serious business to hunt on someone else's land uninvited and where cows are kept.

As it was, he discovered someone had stolen his hog traps. It appeared the thieves came in from a side road, unseen and unheard, which was easy in this isolated area.

I went the next day to see Tippy. She was wobbly, but she was up and wagging that silly tail when she had heard my voice.

The doctor said I could take her home. He gave me the bullet and told me to feed her lightly, keep her warm, and to give her a few days of rest to help her recover. He had put a cone around her neck so she couldn't chew her stitches out. Then he said to bring her back in a few days and he'd take them out.

She and I rode home a little uneasily. I was afraid she would fall off the seat. But no, and as we neared the house, she wagged her tail. She knew she was home and it was something to behold, an animal knowing where home was. We both did.

~ ~ ~

After Tippy had her stitches out, she kind of laid around for a while. But being the little survivor she was, in a couple of weeks she was back chasing squirrels. She was almost 18 years old when I had to have her put down.

I was a little worried about putting her red sweater on her. I was afraid she would get tangled in the brush. Sammy wore hers and stayed around the house. We spent the rest of winter quietly.

I would go clean The Postman's house and would find The Pill Heads sitting around there. I ignored them, but I warned him they would be trouble.

He was recovering some of his financial losses and was feeling better. He would come get me to go for groceries in case he had problems and we'd stop and eat. He loved shrimp. He didn't eat very well, but had survived for so many years doing what he did.

Early morning in early spring can be pretty chilly. The wind would cut into you. Before production would start, he and I would figure out what we needed, make a list, and be ready. I cleaned out the barn and together, we would move the splitters so we could change the plugs and oil and check the hydraulic fluid.

Over the winter, I had gotten a rug latching kit and made a very nice rug for my feet. It was quiet work and I ate and rested as much as one could.

I cleaned my two rain barrels, then stabilized my rain catchment system using some knotted up butts I brought home that I could brace it up with. I kept heating water, trying to stay ahead of things. I still washed dishes, and myself, outside.

The Boys had built me a work-bench kind of dish washing center with a dropped-in sink and I had rebuilt my sauna and bathed out there. I only had a few scorpions around – that was a relief. But my old stove in my Someday Kitchen was my saving grace. When I came home, I could cook and eat in the house. Being able to warm up helped me rest better. Mac and cheese became my new friend. Life was a bit easier.

I wondered how our forefathers and mothers survived. They didn't have automatic water at hand. Many times they'd have to dig a well immediately. They often had to use mealy flour and grains, sifting out the bugs and eating it anyway. Meat soured. And they didn't have a closet full of clothes. Wet was wet and many died from the exposure.

I planted some rose bushes. They were end-of-the-season finds at Walmart and were half dead, but they took to my dirt. I fed them rose food and banana skins. Roses love bananas.

I hand dug my garden this year and my little plants came up. Two weeks later they fell over. My soil was too alkali. If there's an evergreen tree around, you have alkali soil. I wanted to haul in soil for a small raised bed, but my hours would not allow for too intense gardening. I came across some big black containers that I would use to grow some tomatoes, green onions, eggplant, and squash. I could move them to the sun and out of the wind.

That winter I got my first of many doses of disturbed skunks under the house. The dogs would smell them and growl or bark and oh, that was the wrong thing to do. I couldn't make the dogs understand why, though.

~ ~ ~

The days went from bright and sunny to rainy and very cold. The ole house was one of the biggest challenges I faced. I spent the winter putting plastic on the walls and had to go outside to double cover the windows because the wind whistled through them.

The house sat on rocks that had been gathered from the area. They were big and heavy and I could tell they had been manually leveled. I could imagine the man gathering them, making them fit his purpose. That was one of the amazing things about the ole house – it had functioned as a home.

As the chinaberry tree grew, it continued to push on the side of the ole house, but the house resisted. It was a fight of wills in nature.

It was amazing the things I could find to occupy my time. I read so many books, darned my clothes, and made simple curtains by hand. I

100

wrote a lot of letters, ordered catalogs by the dozens, and found my muslin hand towels in a Lehman's catalog. I still have six of them to this day.

We had a real cold spell. I would bank up the burner, which was a science in itself. Oak-butt knots were my friends. That February, I woke to Tippy growling. She never did that or barked. That woke up Sammy and the two boys who slept close to the wood burner.

First, I heard the noise under the house, and then I smelled it. Skunks. Oh my word. The sickening, putrid smell seeped right through the old floor. It was too late to quiet the dogs. That was one time I wished they would have slept through an invasion.

The windows were covered so I had to open the doors to ease the smell. That smell will gag you and make you so sick to your stomach. My goodness it was cold. I threw on my jacket and shoes and stood at the door trying to breathe but I wasn't going outside. I didn't know where the skunks were. And what would I do if they came out from under the house?

There was only one thing to do. I'd have to fix the bottom of the house, board it up so nothing could crawl under it. But first, the smell had to wear-off. Thank goodness my clothes were in the chest. Everything else had to be pulled out and aired. Before I could gather up enough scrap wood to close off the bottom of the house, they would spray four more times.

The side of the house the burner was on sat down close to the ground. The new side was higher. I'd start closing in at the back and front.

I drove into town that morning to get all the mothballs I could. As I closed off the bottom I threw mothballs under the house. It was kinda like herding bees across the Trinity River with a fly swatter. Geezz. As it warmed up, the skunks left and I really went to work. I also had to get a yard rake to get the mothballs out. The smell from them was also pretty strong.

I had asked The Postman to help me rip some stakes and I barred every inch of the bottom. But there was a problem. There must have been a possum under there and it must have died. Lord, I wondered if the wildlife was bent on stinking me out of the house. The smell was so bad I was gagging. I would air the house during the day. It took a while, but finally it went away.

That spring, I would have the family out for an early Easter celebration. We would be back in production soon.

Texas springs are usually fickle, but this year it was beautiful. The boys brought two campers. All the girls knew about the scorpions and snakes and such and they couldn't bring themselves to sleep in sleeping bags on the floor. I had to laugh, but I didn't blame them. The girls did learn to use my solar shower, though. They loved the rain water because their hair would be so squeaky clean and shiny after they washed their hair with it.

We cooked breakfast outside and played Wahoo by firelight in the backyard. The kids fished in the pond. Of course, us old folks who got up early got to see the deer in the meadow and watch the day come alive. It was a very peaceful time, with campfire coffee and family talk. The boys would play horseshoes and we ladies would boil Easter eggs. Of course, the teens got into the spirit. We hid eggs for them to hunt and it was funny to watch, what with fifty acres to hide them in. Middle Son took the kids to the big creek to swim, but it was cold and the city came out in the kids. They didn't stay in long. I had to laugh.

My Oldest Son told me he was headed to Minnesota to work and he asked me a sad question – could he have Charley Brown? Charley had taken to him. If he went to his truck, Charley would jump right in.

Downtown Charley Brown would go to Minnesota. He is buried there, put down after he got very sick. He gave me years of comfort, that tiny, abandoned baby. He was a beautiful collie and I was devastated when I learned he was gone. Oldest Son spent a lot of money trying to save him, but they couldn't. Charley was a South Texas dog but loved the snow. He played in it like Sammy played in the pond.

It was time for production and I needed to get back in shape. It usually took about a week to get my lungs back to my schedule and about two weeks for my body. This would be one of the heaviest of all seasons I worked there. It would bring news my Mother had a heart attack and was in congestive heart failure.

She worked for the Florida Highway patrol in the driver's license division. They had a senior program and she loved the job, giving the oral driver's license exam to those who couldn't read.

She and I were never very close, but I loved her, and would grieve what we didn't have.

~ ~ ~

I had carefully stocked up on canned foods. I could cook my lunch when I cooked my supper, then put it in my cooler and transfer it to The Postman's fridge until lunch.

I still bought my sweet rolls. They were my only snack food. I once tried pudding packs but couldn't handle the processed taste.

Meat was still stored in the Postman's freezer on his back porch, but I didn't have that much to put in there, which turned out to be a good thing when The Postman bought a beef half and needed a lot of the space to store it.

Later, as the season got started, Fake Fanny returned, as arrogant and hateful as ever. She was so pompous, acting as if she was the Queen returning to her kingdom, as if nothing had happened. She never suffered any repercussions and denied she had taken the funds.

I wondered why The Postman didn't file charges so I asked him. He said he didn't really know what to do. She always managed the books and order-delivery scheduling. I believed he was scared, too. I know he was so afraid of losing his place and felt as if he was dammed if he did hold her accountable and dammed if he didn't.

It would start to take a serious toll on his health. He became depressed and short-tempered and wasn't sleeping well. He was still eating, though many times when I would need something for the woodpile and go to the house, he would be asleep in his chair.

I truly wanted to choke those two brats. What a change a thorough beating might have made.

The Mexicans and I remembered having to wait for our money and the ugly way she treated us, so she was way down on our list. But she was The Egos wife, so we had no say in the matter, and shouldn't, I suppose. But her treating people like so much trash stuck in my craw then and still does to this day.

We all knew she considered us beneath her, but at the same time, she and The Ego needed us. It seemed like a Catch-22 situation. For our part, I needed the job and the Mexicans had families to feed. At times I would leave so aggravated, I swore to myself on the way home that I wouldn't go back. But come morning, I would be up, building a fire, making coffee, and cussing myself. What could I do but hang on?

~ ~ ~

The Mexicans and I ignored the Block Buster. We had two Husky and two Stihl chain saws. We favored the Stihls. I would pull the bar while they tightened or changed out the chains. Those chains were changed out often. Dirt ain't their friend and they dulled quickly cutting through logs on the ground.

The Huskys stayed in the shop. They were big, heavy monsters with long bars and bigger chains and their chains were expensive. It took forever to sharpen them, even on the electric sharpener.

At least The Ego finally got off his rear and cut us some butts. We pulled the splitters out in the sun because it was colder than usual and we had a long way to go.

The splitters were an amazing bunch of machines. We carefully watched the oil and could lay them down and move them in minutes.

We did our best to keep our work area as clean as possible. You have all kinds of scraps coming off the butts and if you had to get up and move around, you had to be very careful. People were throwing wood in piles from different directions. There was a rhythm to it all and you would soon get into it.

When new guys came in, it was almost funny watching them try to get it, to figure out the rhythm. I would have my Spanish-speaking guy tell them to go slow, be careful, and watch their thumbs.

One thing about those who didn't speak English – they watched everything I did. If I kicked a butt into the bottom of a wedge, they did it. If I got up to clean my area, they did, too. They wanted to learn, and they did.

There were black-widow spiders, scorpions, and other critters in the wood. We had to constantly watch out for everything. I learned to stuff my pant legs into my socks and put rubber bands on them. I didn't want any critters crawling up my pants.

There was always one person who cooked. The men all pitched in for their food, like chorizo and eggs with flour tortillas and lots of bananas. They brought a little cooking kit with a skillet and paper plates.

We still had the old wood burner in the barn and we would fire it up in the morning, but it didn't really warm it much. I think it was just a mind game. We thought we were getting warm so we felt warmer.

I brought down one of my campfire coffee pots and we kept coffee going all day. The work could be rough and the caffeine kept us sharp. I had a good crew and the guys never questioned me, though that would be tested further on in the season. I thought how strange it was that they looked to me to keep our peaceful working conditions. We had suffered through fighting for our money, the weather, and some of the owners and their friends. But they knew Annie wouldn't let them down.

I believe to this day we had a working bond as strong as any crew could have had regardless of racial or ethnic makeup. Their showing up every day to the woodpile helped me keep a job that fed me and my critters. Without them, I don't know where I would have been.

~ ~ ~

As I write this, I have days I try to let you know how it really was. But sometimes I have to stop for a few days. This is the most personal thing I have ever done and sometimes it feels overwhelming.

I try to write a lot about the details of what happened, hoping it might make this story more personal to you or give you a better understanding of my walk, of things like beginning to be lonely as the years passed and thinking of having someone in my life. I don't know. My life was one of survival. I didn't have time to develop a relationship and besides, the pickings were slim in the woods.

Only once did I even come close to letting it happen and he wasn't from this country. I knew he was interested in me from the way he looked at me, from the way he would rush to help me with the very heavy wood butts and move my splitter for me. You know when you know.

He was tall, graying, and very quiet spoken. My English speaking hand told me, "He likes you."

He was my age, but when I would think of my little life on my fifty acres, I didn't know how to share it with anyone. It was such a private walk, a journey I couldn't expect another soul to understand. Nor expect them to live it with me.

It was a hard time for me. He was a good, hardworking man. That was never the problem. And I didn't have any problems with his race or his world. Just with letting him live in mine.

It was such a selfish, spiritual walk I was on and I didn't know how to explain it to him, or even to myself.

~ ~ ~

My Mother was recovering from her heart attack. I was able to talk to her because The Postman had made it clear I was to use his phone to keep in touch with my family.

I was dumbfounded to learn what had brought on the heart attack. My niece, my sister's adopted daughter, had died in a house fire. Because the fire has been under investigation for many years, I won't discuss it other than to say she died under very suspicious circumstances. It was heart-breaking news. I would cry many times over it, knowing what I knew and what my Mother suspected. She had told me about it, but she couldn't get past it.

Then I learned my sister-in-law of almost thirty years had developed colon cancer. My brother married her while he was in the Army stationed in Germany.

Life goes on though. Every morning was a trial, especially getting logs. Things came to a standstill with no butts to split. But the men and I were not loggers. Logging is a dangerous job. I was a firm believer that cutting down a tree was the most dangerous thing you could be involved in. Being killed in the woods doing that was not going to happen to me.

I waited until The Ego woke up that morning. I would have a talk with him.

I was paid to make The Postman money and I took the job seriously. The Fake Fanny went off on one of her shopping trips so it was a good time for a discussion.

I asked to speak to him. I was going to try and reach him. We had good people on the woodpile, faithfully returning season after season. We were making them money and to fuss at us because there were no pallets on the yard was unreasonable. It was out of our control.

We talked for a few minutes and suddenly he got to his mother dying. I listened and it came to me – he had not really grieved. He was the youngest but his family had never talked about the Mother's death.

I told him what had worked for me – to just go forward. It seemed that morning, he and I finally jelled. He didn't know how to grieve. I didn't either, but I understood.

He didn't know any of the men. I told him he didn't know me either and to come out to the barn and let me introduce him to everyone. That evening as we wound down production, he came out with beer for the guys and through our English-speaking man, he talked to them.

The next morning we had a surprise. He was up and dragging logs to us!

That season we would deal with the Forestry people. They told us there had to be one-hundred percent hardwood in the bundles. No pine. I was left to explain to them that hardwood was all we ever put in our bundles.

We would be inspected and our bundles would be measured for so much footage and type of wood many times. Apparently, there were some renegade woodpiles opening up and they weren't following the rules. In East Texas, Forest Management rules.

That season I had at least ten men working, and then came the block-buster race. I loved it.

I lost a lot of weight working the woodpile. I had weighed between 150-160 pounds and I got down to about 117 ponds and it was all muscle. I was in the best physical shape of my life. But I was still getting older. I wondered how long a fifty-something woman could maintain the pace and the work.

On a trip to the Walmart one day, I saw something I had passed many times, so I wheeled into the junk-yard. The owner came out. I asked him what he was going to do with that old, 10' x 50' mobile home. He said he planned to make a store room out of it. I told him I wanted to buy it and asked him how much he wanted for it.

"Five hundred dollars," he said.

Done! Now I had to get it dragged to the house.

A fellow had a tire shop/wrecker service. On my way back, I stopped and asked him if he'd haul it for me. He told me, "Yep, for fifty dollars."

I almost fell over. Boy was that cheap.

I knew I would have to pull my gate and connecting side fences down to get it in the yard and wished I had some help. Then, voilà, my Middle Son showed up that night.

He asked, "Why is it every time I come to visit, you have something needs doing?"

Giving him the mama smile, I told him, "You're just lucky I guess."

The Road was narrow, and the tow driver would have to get a curving run at my driveway. By the time I got home the next night, she was sitting in my drive.

My plan was to put her behind the house, but *that* would never happen.

The $500 mobile that would one day become my home.

~ ~ ~

There were some things that terrified me. The Block Buster was one of them. I think it was originally designed for home milling logs for housing.

Before the logs could be loaded, they had to be debarked, which was extra work. Then the forklift had to lift logs on to it. The saw was set to a twenty-two inch cut so that when logs ran through it, they were cut into twenty-two inch butts, then forced into a four-way wedge. Of course, logs would jam up whether they were twenty-two inches or fifty feet long. That meant the Block Buster had to be shut down and the butts unlocked, which was not easy. When jammed together, wood settles into itself. The pieces literally grab hold of each other. A pile of butts would do it overnight. If it rained, they would swell and be even harder to unlock.

As I mentioned earlier, nobody wanted to use the thing. Finally, we decided I would race the Block Buster and if I won they would get rid of it. The deal was that I was to put out as many butts as the monster Block Buster. We agreed on how many piles of butts and how high and a time limit of two hours.

The Postman made a mark on the barn for the height of the piles. Normal stuff so far. They had four guys on the Block Buster and I had one loading log butts for me and my good saw hand cutting mine into standard twenty-two inch butts. I had moved my splitter out into the fresh air.

Right up front, the Block Buster was a waste of man-power. And it wouldn't run for more than thirty to forty minutes without a shut down. The man who owned the Block Buster came out and swore by the miserable monster. He charged $800 a month to rent it.

It wasn't cockiness or ego or anything. I just knew I could do it and I loved the job. The Postman was worried. He kept telling me I didn't have to do this and kept saying I was going to hurt myself. I wasn't worried, though.

My heart rate would be one that I have never achieved again. It pumped like a prize fighter's. My splitter was in great shape and it was cool and sunny. I warmed up with a few butts then told my loader to just keep me loaded. We had about the same size logs. I asked him to please not whack me on the shin 'cause, believe it or not, it really hurts when a green butt slaps you.

I can remember beginning and starting easy, steady, and relaxed. My pile was not making an impression until I called on my adrenaline and pushed harder and the wood started flying. I remember The Ego's wife, Fake Fanny, hollering for me to stop, that I was going to kill myself.

The Block Buster had to be stopped to get a log jam undone. I had a jump on the machine now. I thought I should back off a bit but I couldn't. I had an adrenaline surge and it had to burn off. My muscles started to burn and the back of my head was tightening up, but I just kept pushing for the whole two hours.

The Mexicans grinned and stayed back. My saw hand never stopped and my loader had to move to keep butts within my reach.

I remember hearing the Block Buster shut down, and then The Postman kept tapping me on the shoulder. Time was up I had five piles of logs to the Block Buster's three. Most of the piles were at six feet tall.

The Block Buster owner did not say a word. The Ego told him he could take the Block Buster with him.

What I accomplished was to prove that evil machine wasn't near as efficient as humans. It took more men to load and take care of it than I did.

I'd won, but I couldn't move. It was as if my muscles were locked up. The Postman brought me some pickle juice. I thought he was nuts, but he all but ordered me to drink it. And I knew I had to walk to get my heart rate down. When you have that much adrenaline in your blood, you can't just stop like that. It took me about an hour to cool down. Then, suddenly, I felt like a newborn baby, weak-kneed and shaky.

The Postman was right. The pickle juice really helped. I thought for sure I would have charley horses after all that, but I didn't.

The men just grinned and I gave them a wink. We did it. We had been working in this place for a long time now and had always done what we were asked. I knew the men would have quit if they had to run that machine. And if I remember correctly, that particular model was recalled.

There was beer all round to celebrate, except for me. I didn't drink alcohol anymore. I just climbed in the old truck and headed home.

I had done something that day that proved my worth, which proved no matter our age, men and women all have another place inside us we can call on to do amazing things. You just have to dig down for it.

When I got to the gate, I could have sworn the ole House smiled. I wasn't going to make any more money and there was no promotion for beating the machine, but I had more respect for myself.

That night, as I sat with my coffee cooking on my beautiful old stove, I remembered how far I had come. Living on sweet-rolls, dealing with rats and scorpions and snakes, my Tippy nearly killed, freezing to death, feeling lost and disappointed with myself, but never with my decision to live here. I was truly at home.

Sometimes that only happens once in a lifetime.

~ ~ ~

It never ceases to amaze me what I could and couldn't live without. The only thing I truly missed was my blow dryer. I didn't need make-up but I had to have lotions.

I learned that a tennis ball was a perfect bath-tub stopper and that a sock secured with a rubber band was the perfect cover to keep critters and dirt out of my gun barrels.

I learned water was my main source of life and that using bleach in my dish water and water heating tubs and rain barrels kept me alive and safe from bacteria.

I learned to always have a full tank of gas and how to live without people around me.

I learned to live without noise, cold milk, or lots of meat.

I became frantic about learning and books were my tools. I couldn't read enough and never had enough books.

Creature comforts became what I made them. I learned to do without and live without so many things. But I couldn't live without my God. Praying became my refuge.

I will continue to pray for everyone who wants the off-grid life. If you're there, trying to get there, or you're just dreaming about it now, never give up your dream, even if you have to backtrack, regroup where you're at, or just plain start over.

It may be difficult, but Annie knows you can do it. I know you can.

~ ~ ~

When I first went off grid, the days seem to drag. They seemed never-ending with all I had to do while trying to make it work.

I was always securing my water and keeping tubs going.

Food was a shock at first, learning there would be no big meals. I didn't cook them in the summer because there was no way to keep leftovers from spoiling. Winter was different. The cold nights were the only way I could keep food overnight that would not fit in my little ice chest.

The years were slipping by now. I had figured out that by buying a case of the small cans of evaporated milk, I could have a bowl of cereal. I ate cereal many times at night, too, when I was too tired from being in the woodpile all day to cook.

I would buy large packs of pork chops and split them up and put them in the freezer at The Postman's. And on the weekends, I would eat as much as I could. I suppose I didn't use that freezer as much as I could have. I really tried to keep my business on the other end of the road. My end.

The summer before my Mother died, we were up to seventeen hands at the woodpile, including me and the Sad Little Guy. We had more orders coming in.

Just getting The Ego and his wife out of bed was The Postman's big problem. I followed his orders. He let me know how many pallets he needed for the next day and we would go for it as long as we had the logs on the ground.

He and I would meet in the barn before daylight. I personally checked the oil in the splitters and make sure they were full of gas. The Postman would fill me in on the day's happenings and we'd just plain ole gossip about what was happening in the small town and what was happening with NASCAR. He had become a fiend for car racing. Then, when the men came in, he'd go listen to all the news and listen for the telephone, for orders.

One morning he came out and asked me to go listen for the phone and take any orders that came in. He had to run into town and get the Pill Heads. They had gone for cigarettes and sodas and passed out while pulling out of the store parking lot into the middle of a very busy road and run off into a ditch.

The store owner knew who they were and called The Postman. When he got there, they were wasted – past wasted really. They didn't know where they were and didn't know what was happening. He got them in his truck and brought them back to his house. Then he called the girl's mother. She asked him to get somebody to bring her car back home and thanked him.

They had both been to rehab many times, but legal scripts from many doctors kept them in pills. He was drawing SSI and she was on food stamps.

I had so much work to do and The Postman had such an investment in this little business that we didn't have time for their nonsense. The day came when he had taken the girl for her methadone and she was beyond standing up. She wandered into the barn and almost gave me a heart attack when she walked up behind my saw hand as he was cutting butts. He had no idea she was there and could have killed her with the saw. We always gave him his space and never, ever walked up behind him.

One of the men jumped and grabbed her and flung her away from him and she started screaming. Well, that shut us down. The Postman heard her and came running. I told him what had happened and begged him not to let her come back out here. It could have been horrible.

I shut us down for an early break. The men were scared to death, afraid they'd be blamed, but there was no way I would have let that happen. They saved her. We had some coffee and snacks and when everybody was settled back down, we went back to work.

The woodpile was a very dangerous place and an accident could kill you in a heartbeat.

A few months later, The Pill Heads ventured into Houston and had a wreck. She refused medical help and he was just beat up a bit. Her stepfather brought them home. The next morning when her boyfriend got up, she wasn't in bed. He found her on the floor. She had bled from the brain and drowned in her own blood and died. What a mess. He went back to live with his mother in The Heights in Houston and two weeks later choked on a sandwich and died.

Such a sad waste of life.

~ ~ ~

We averaged 24 to 30 pallets a day. Most days, The Ego would make one run, but at times, short trips meant he could haul two loads. Only twelve pallets could be loaded on the low-boy. He had to take the pallet jack with him so there wasn't room for more.

We hadn't had any rain and things were getting pretty dry. Before that summer was over, I would see my cistern drop ten to twelve feet.

I was in panic mode. I still washed dishes but only had a solar shower or a short bath every three days. It got very bad, with fire bans all through the counties.

I bought two more six-gallon water cans from Walmart. I now had eight. I don't know how to make anyone understand how important water is off-grid. If you never read another word about self-reliance, think water – where's it at and how to get it.

On grid, as long as your bill is paid, water runs freely out of the faucet. Off-grid, especially during a drought, you sometimes dream about having a water bill.

One day, a weekend warrior came out and decided to burn a stump and then go off and leave it. I was home and had smelled the smoke and was already worried, but I got really spooked when the fire trucks went past the house. I jumped in the truck and headed down there to help. This far out, everybody's a volunteer firefighter.

The fire had run all the way to The Postman's fence line, probably a hundred yards from his house. The Ego was already firing up the bulldozer. The Postman had wet blankets and was trying to help but he didn't look too good. Thank God the daughter-in-law got him in the house. Everything on his place was at stake, his home and all the equipment. We fought and fought. The fire trucks had to refill out of his pond then turn and come back.

Time and again, just as we thought it was out, it would pop up again after running under months of dead Bahia grass. Finally the dozer was able to give us a good fire break and we let it burn out to the dirt.

I was black from head to toe and felt as nasty as I looked. Smoke was in my throat, my nose, and my hair and my clothes were ruined.

The fire had burned about five hundred acres, but didn't touch the idiot's house who set the stump on fire. But he got a big ticket. It was a no-burn ban violation ticket with a big fine.

The thing about neighbors out here in the country is that we pretty much keep to ourselves. But come crisis time, we're always there to help.

I thought maybe, just maybe, I had repaid some of The Postman's kindnesses. He wasn't well and old folks don't deal well with this type of threat and stress.

~ ~ ~

It was late summer. We split wood from morning 'till dark.

In September, on my birthday, The Postman took me to town to eat. He wanted shrimp, and my birthday was a good excuse. It was a nice time, but unusual, and I felt out of place. After we ate, we got our groceries and went home to The Road. It always felt so peaceful to go through the gate.

I was still putting stuff away when I heard him honking. I thought I must have forgotten something. When I went out, he looked strange and told me to come down to his place and call my Mother's house.

My sister answered. She said Mother was in the hospital with pneumonia and very sick. I asked her if I should come out, but she told to wait and see, that the doctor was optimistic. But her heart was his real concern. I told her the hours I worked and to call me when she had any word.

Two days later, we had stopped production and were cleaning up when The Postman came out and told me to call my sister. The pneumonia was caused by a rare, very fast moving cancer. This was on a Tuesday. She said the doctor didn't think she'd make the weekend, probably not later than Friday. It was that fast.

I can't fly and had no one to take me to Houston anyway. So I asked The Postman if he'd take me to the bus station. Back then, you could get straight-through buses.

I ran home, split the sack of dog food open, and put down as much water as I could for Tippy and Sammy. Then I took a fast, cold, solar bath and threw some clothes in a bag.

I left late that night and got to Florida Wednesday afternoon. We all lived a long way off. Mother had moved to Florida on her own. The only one who couldn't make it was my youngest brother.

Mother died Friday night. She asked to be cremated. My brother sent me my share of her ashes, which will be buried with me when I pass on.

That part of my life will never be finished. Things left unsaid...fences un-mended.

When I got back Sunday night, my friend was there to pick me up. I remember standing at the gate. It was dark and he waited until I unlocked the house before he headed home. My girls were about to pop. They needed to go outside real bad.

I had a doll that I had taken. Mother collected them. She had about three hundred. My baby sister had already taken everything of value. All I had asked for a long time before was the old family photo album with pictures from the 1800's. She had taken them too.

The doll was old, what is called *The Spanish Dancer*. That night, I curled up with that doll and cried myself to sleep. I still have it.

I learned at an early age to suck it up and go on, but there was a place in me that was angry and my sister had things to answer for. She had waited so late to call us because she was cleaning out the house and Mother wasn't even gone yet.

One day she will answer, to One a whole lot more powerful than I am, for her greed and selfishness, for her adopted daughter who had died very mysteriously in a fire, for everything. One day it will all be answered for.

I gave myself another day to rest and recover then went back to work. I had to work off the anger.

~ ~ ~

It's strange to me now, as I'm looking back.

While I was bailing water out of the ground, other ladies were getting manicures and their hair done. While I was sharpening my axe, hatchet, and snake-killing hoe, they were shopping at the Mall.

That was their life and great for them! I know shopping can be fun, but so can finding security in life.

The drought continued. My rain barrel was dry and the water level in my cistern was dropping.

The Postman would take my kegs in and fill them when he went for gas. I couldn't get water from him. Although he had huge filters on his well, he had skunk water – it soured if it sat too long. It was nasty stuff and the smell...wow!

One Sunday as I did my chores, I was putting away my laundry when I opened my sock drawer and thought, *I don't have socks that color*. As I focused on the pattern it dawned on me...snake!!

It was a young rattlesnake. With the drought, mice had been

coming in for food and water. Tippy would make short order of the ones she could catch but she didn't catch them all. Apparently, the mice attracted the snake. It scared the dickens out of me!

It sounded its rattle and I backed away. Calling the girls, I put them outside in case it got away from me. Then I reached in by the door and grabbed the machete. I was going to have to be fast, very fast. It was already coiled up and striking was a split second thing for rattlers.

I took the blade in both hands and eased to the side. Then I plunged the machete in at its head and bam! Got it. But that snake thrashing around in my sock drawer was not a nice thing. I eased the drawer out and carefully looked behind it and under it. One snake often means there's more. Oh Lord, I hoped not.

Fortunately, I didn't find any more after turning the big chest over and checking. But now I had to watch for rattlers in the house, and pray the dogs didn't find one.

Until it rained and the critters went back to the woods I would keep the girls in and they didn't like that. They had an all-day ritual of hunting and Sammy swimming in the pond.

Production went well that fall. I was dealing with Mom's death and the lawyers and paper work. And we slid into winter and coolness.

As we came to the year 2000, I began to hear about Y2K. If it hadn't been for *Backwoods Home Magazine*, I wouldn't even have known it was a possibility. I decided to close my little bank account and reinforced my hidey hole. And I ramped up my stored food and supplies. Of course, it turned out to be nothing much, but having extra food and supplies on-hand is never a bad thing.

I had been making my wheat bread. I tried rye, but the dogs wouldn't even play with it. And I found other things to do after production that winter.

In November, my oldest brother was killed in a work-related accident. He had been electrocuted by a bare 220-volt wire rubbing an air conditioning unit as he undid the underpinning on a mobile home they were moving. I remember crashing to my knees and thinking, *Lord God, what next?*

Once again I got on a bus, this time, to Georgia. I was devastated. I had to say good-bye to him.

There were people there I didn't know, including a young couple with a three-year-old, little-doll of a girl. Only hours before the accident, she had been playing, running around that A/C unit and climbing on it. The folks said they were so sorry. But he had probably saved her life in giving his.

My sister-in-law would follow him to the grave within a few weeks, dying of colon cancer. Two months later my brother-in-law would drop dead of a heart attack at work. His was the fourth family death in a year.

I think I went kinda blank that winter, just working and coming home. I walked the woods and saw the old doe, but she was alone. No fawns. She didn't get up. Just stayed laying in the brush. She knew I belonged there, as she did. I watched her for a while. With all that had happened, being there with her helped me, reminded me that there was still some normalcy in my world.

I sat down on a log and for the first time, screamed at God and all the miserable things going on. But life is life. It happens and we can't change it, no matter how much we want to.

Eventually, spring would come again and I could go to the woodpile and work until things didn't hurt so bad.

That winter the rains finally came. My barrels filled up and my cistern overflowed again. It was good to see.

I welcomed the cold. The snakes were hibernating and the ole burner kept us warm again. I read when I wasn't doing all the survival maintenance. I call it "survival" now, but of course it was just my normal way of living then.

Time passed.

For the first time, as I snuggled up with a book and, yeah, some sweet rolls, I realized how cozy things had gotten in my little home. And I figured out something. God tries those whom he loves. *Well*, I thought, *you are a razor sharp sword so don't let these lessons go to waste.*

Spring production would start and we would have three MS13 [Mara Salvatrucha] gang members show up to work. We had to be very careful our regular Mexicans would tell me.

Muy malo. Muy, muy malo. Very bad. Very, very bad.

~ ~ ~

The MS13 gangs were beginning to come into the States and were known for their murderous ways.

Early in the fall, my men showed up with another car behind them. My English speaking Mexican shook his head, kind of as a heads up.

Three guys got out of the second car. They all had red do-rags on their heads and acted arrogant with a kind of swaggering bravado.

I turned my back to them so they couldn't see me talking to my guy and asked him what they wanted. He said their gang name in Spanish, addressing me as Señora and the other guys as hombres and said, "Muy malo." They were gang members and nephews to a man in town.

I told him to tell them to wait. I had the other men go ahead and start working then went in to talk to The Postman.

We had a problem. As best as I could understand, they had weapons in the car. I told him they wanted our regulars to give them their jobs and were serious trouble. The Postman called our Constable, who asked which road they came in on. We told him the back way and he said he would set up a roadblock on the front side and to tell them to come back early in the morning.

They wanted them bad. They had caused trouble in Huntsville – a really dumb thing to do. They were likely to end up on death row in the Bluebird Motel, which was what we called the prison because the buses that brought prisoners to the penitentiary were blue.

So I gathered up myself and went out to ask my man to translate. I told him to tell them I needed them to come back tomorrow, early in the morning, when we would have more wood. The Postman gave me ten dollars to give them for gas.

If you know about the MS13 gangs you know they are killers and dope dealers and have no qualms about killing you. We smiled and I told my man to be happy and tell them we'd have work for them tomorrow and to give them the money for gas so they'd be okay and think we were all okay with them.

They piled back into the car and off they went.

I learned later they had been arrested when they came off the old road. They were wanted out of San Angelo for robbery and murder.

119

Geezz...talk about a close call.

My Mexican translator said they had threatened them. My hands were documented, decent, hard-working men. They weren't cowards but they weren't stupid either.

In the fall, I would get my first cell phone. It was as big as a box of kitchen matches and it was a circus trying to get bars enough to call. If I need to call the kids, I had to drive to the end of The Road and stand up in the back of the truck. It wasn't funny then, but now I find it hilarious. I also had a ten-foot ladder in the meadow. I would climb up as high as I could go without it turning over and sometimes I could call out. Sometimes.

My house was more comfortable. I enjoyed making bread, kneading it on my old table, letting it rise in the living room by the wood burner.

I would take Sammy to the pond and let her swim while Tippy hunted rabbits. Times like that were priceless.

I was in love with a way of life and it loved me back.

~ ~ ~

I mentioned before that during these years I read so many books. I got caught up in Tom Clancy's novels. He's a fascinating writer. I've re-read each of his books many times, even to this day. It was in *The Sum Of All Fears* that I found my motto: *Trouble Rides A Fast Horse*.

On September 11, 2001, I woke to the world on fire. It was my sixtieth birthday. When I woke up, I turned on my cell phone and had a voice mail from my daughter. It was an emergency. I went to the pasture, got on the ladder, and called her. At that time, information was sketchy, but she told me, "Momma they have bombed New York."

My mind screamed self-defense. I jumped in the truck, headed to our little feed store, and bought all the ammo he had for my pistol and shotgun. Everyone was stunned. They had a little television on and we watched, horrified, as people jumped many stories to their deaths to keep from burning to death. They re-showed the planes hitting the Twin Towers. Sheer terror griped me.

I pushed the ole truck hard to the house. I needed to get some money from my hidey-hole. Then I went to the little Walmart and bought flour, sugar, and canned meat – Treet and Spam. I had bread making yeast but got extra. I bought two cases of canned milk, extra dog food, and lamp oil, even though I had good supply. I bought jelly, peanut butter, beans, and extra D-cell batteries and headed home

When I got in the house and finished putting all my purchases away, I started shaking. I was born into war. There had been little peace. I remember thinking *Dear God, not this country again.*

I hid the truck in the back, put blankets on the windows to block out any light from escaping from the lamps, and both guns were always loaded.

I took the extra ammo to my hidey hole. I knew that spot like the back of my hand and knew I could find it in the dark. It was at a dry creek and deep enough for cover. I honestly didn't know what was going on, but whatever it was, I wanted to be prepared.

I turned on my radio trying to figure out what *was* going on and called the kids. I told them if it is a war, to come to me and to bring water and sleeping bags and whatever groceries that could. No matter what happened, we'd be okay. The boys had their own arsenals.

By that time, I had forgotten it was my birthday, and so had everyone else. It was a long time before I ever celebrated it.

Finally as the days went by, I got the whole story that hijackers had rammed the Twin Towers and the Pentagon in huge planes. And I learned about the brave folks who took the fourth plane away from the killers and gave their lives when it crashed to save thousands of other lives.

I also learned something else, something important. I always knew I needed to save money, but now I realized I also needed to be better prepared.

I had to save money for the down time because seasonal work is short. But so is life if you don't get ready for emergencies and disasters.

I wasn't going to leave. I had fought hard for this place and it was my home. If it was time, if we were at war again, surviving here couldn't be worse than some of the things I had already gone through.

I knew to stay dark at night. I knew where I was and they didn't. To this day, I still hear those words – *we are at war.* At the time, I didn't even know who we were at war with. Nor had I heard of jihadist Muslims or even what jihad was. I didn't know Osama bin Laden even existed.

Then I got mad. How dare they threaten my Country? How dare they kill innocent people who were just going about lives? I would stand my ground. I was alone, but I was a totally different person from the woman who'd moved here years before. I had always had the spirit. Now I knew why.

I almost dared them – come and get you some of this. Sheer terror will make you think or die.

I was going to live and this was my home.

~ ~ ~

During the Y2K scare, people had been buying up the available land for sale on The Road. There were many more cars and trucks, and a white van.

I would wake straight up at night at the sound of the new cars. I found it strange that there would be traffic that late at night so I would get up and watch the road. These were not the kind of vehicles we were used to. Everybody had trucks. The Road wasn't kind to cars and in the mud, it was a nightmare.

Life continued. The Ego and Fake Fanny were making noise about another business. Oh, rats...what now?

The woodpile continued, but the orders were letting up. We still had contracts to fill and had to fight for logs.

The Postman got in touch with an old friend and started having him bring us hardwoods. He logged pines and the mill he used didn't take hardwoods. The Postman did manage to get The Ego to drag them up to the yard for us.

In November, The Postman came out and said he wanted to talk to me. The Ego and The Fake Fanny were going to lease a small grocery store at the crossroads twenty miles away!

"Why?" I asked. "They don't work this business like they should. It's hit or miss at best." I thought, *oh my God. What are we going to do if The Ego wasn't going to be bringing logs?*

He said we'll go on as long as we can and I told him we could still do hickory or special pallets if we could get the wood.

And then I went for it. I asked him how they got the money to stock the store. He told me they had mortgaged the heavy equipment. I figured that would last for about 6 months.

Then they bought a portable barbecue pit and went into the barbecue business.

In the meantime, they would separate again and again.

I had to tell my men we were going to lay them off. Some had tears in their eyes. We had worked in the most primitive of conditions for years. We kept the two original men for a couple of months. Then it was just me.

Thank God I was receiving my small widow's pension, because things were about to get bad for The Postman. He still owed money on the woodpile operations.

I felt like the wind was knocked out of me. Suddenly I would be back to figuring out what to do.

My probate lawyers were bombarding me with papers to sign.

I was skin and bones, but it was all muscle and I was very strong for my age. I was brown as a burlap sack and so alert that I could catch noises that I never would have heard in the city.

Just before our last pallets of the season, we had fairly nice weather. It was cold but dry and I read that night until my eyes wouldn't stay open.

I went out and brought in some heavy knots to bank the burner with and a white van eased by, slowly. The hair on the back of my neck stood up.

I knew it wasn't right. As I started back in to put my 2x4 brace on the door, I heard the door slide open on the van. My little .25 pistol was on the table by my chair and the shotgun was by my bed. That saved my life, I believe, having to go for it.

I grabbed my fanny pack with my ammo and threw it on. As I grabbed the 20-guage, bullets tore through the door. It wasn't made of the home-milled planks that the house was built from. Bullets pinged off those.

I hit the floor and started to crawl to the back door. I would have to stand up to take the 2x4 brace off the door. I couldn't do that. Staying down, I dragged the long, skinny table away from the kitchen window, then pushed it up until I pushed the screen off. I rolled out of it and ran. They couldn't see me from that angle. I was in hyper-mode and ran so fast until I hit the dry creek with my extra ammo, water, and a blanket.

The shooting stopped but I could still hear the motor on the van. Then, slowly, they idled off. I guess they thought they had gotten me. Then I had a horrible thought – Tippy and Sammi had run under the bed. I prayed that they hadn't hit a lamp. I feared fire and I prayed the girls would stay under the bed but I was wrong. They damned near scared the bejeebers out of me when their cold noses touched me. They had followed me out the window, and cringed next to me, shaking and cold and for the first time, they weren't barking.

I was glad I had stored the small emergency tote by the creek. I wrapped us in a blanket and we lay there quietly. Whoever they were, they didn't know the property. I did, like the back of my hand. We would stay very still.

All the time I had been in my house, I had learned to think ahead. I had found the small tote at a yard sale. It had a tight fitting lid.

I made myself think, if I had to hide, what would I need? Knowing water was my life saver I had put a gallon of water, a light blanket, a small flashlight, and a plastic tube in the tote.

I had read in one of my magazines, *Backwoods Home*, I believe, about taking plastic pipe and gluing a cap on one end and a fitting on the other end with a cap that could be screwed on. In that, I put 20-gauge ammo and a box of shells for the .25 revolver. I had the shotgun shells in a plastic sack, but not closed all the way to leave a breathing hole. I didn't want humidity to build up. I also put in the money I hid since my last break in.

The old dry creek was kind of strange really. It was washed out in some parts with brush and small trees around it. My tote was gray, so you almost had to fall over it to know it was there.

Laying in the dark, I could hear forever. My eyes adapted to the dark quickly because I lived with low light. I almost laughed out loud. I was out-smarting the bad guys. I just wished I wasn't shaking so bad.

I don't know how long it was until I heard the guy with the big, black diesel going out to work.

My keys were in my fanny pack. I eased around to the west, circling the house. I stayed low, listening. The diesel had gone out without slowing up, so there wasn't anyone in the road.

I eased my way in the dark to the back of the house, where I always parked the truck to unload my scrap wood in piles, and the girls hopped in. The gate was an obstacle. It was chained and locked. Carefully, I made my way out to the front to unlock and open the gate, then hurried back to my truck. I would go to The Postman's. He would be up, usually by four anyway.

I didn't know that old truck had wings, but it did. I flew down the road. I was honking as I got to his house and he came out. I told him what happened and he was on the phone immediately with the Sheriff.

~ ~ ~

The Postman wanted me to stay at his house. I thought about it, but I had to say no. I had survived, many days, months, and years at my place and I wanted to go home. If you were there, you might have thought I had lost my mind. I was sitting there thinking, *ain't nobody running me off my front porch.*

The Sheriffs' Deputy came on the run along with my old Constable friend.

The Deputy asked me all the questions as the Constable listened. Then the Constable nodded for the Deputy to come outside.

When I say the old law men know what's going on, they do. They know who's into doing bad stuff.

The Old Constable said he'd go back to the house with me. He wanted to see if he could pick up any slugs that had bounced off that old home milled dried plank house siding. My goodness it was tough. I had tried to pound in a many a nail and it never worked.

The Constable told me he was sure he knew what was going on. They were going to get warrants for that morning. These meth cookers slept days and shot at people at night. They were cowards – meth-cooking idiots.

He told me to lock up. He could have saved his breath. Of course I'd lock up. Then he looked round outside the gate as it was getting to be daylight. He looked at the van tracks – he had a thing about tracks – remembering the deer poachers. Then he told me he'd be back later and locked the gate on the way out.

I later learned that they were watching these thugs. They had a lot of evidence. It seemed that with all the War on Drugs in the surrounding bigger towns, the meth cookers were moving to the woods. Someone had gotten wise and had smelled the drug cooking. It's a distinctive smell, like cooking cat urine.

I went in, blew out the lamps, and put on water for coffee. Damn, I needed a cup, bad.

My girls, ole Tippy and Sammie, stayed glued to me. I had to kneel down and grab them both and tears came to my eyes. Dadgum it, we had been through a lot together. So far, we had weathered all that came against us – being hungry, cold, so hot, exhausted, at times so very lonely, and snakes and critters of all kinds and they had always been here when I got home, tails wagging, hopping up on me to pet them, and to let me know they loved me.

The Constable would be back later that day, and he was grinning. Old time law men, they know that they know.

He knew.

~ ~ ~

The Constable explained what was going to happen.

They had picked up the van. The driver was asleep as expected, and sweated the thug enough that he gave up the other two. They were on parole and were going back to prison for a long time. The sentence for a convicted felon in possession of weapons, shooting at people, and manufacturing drugs looked like about thirty to forty years.

As for the other one, the driver of the van, he had warrants out for him from Dallas. The Constable said the judge might want to talk to me, but to keep down the possibility of retaliation they would try to keep me out of it. I couldn't identify them anyway, just the van.

How it all happened, was that I was always gone, working in the woodpile, so the only time these guys ever saw me was if it was daylight enough or on the weekends, when I sat on the front porch reading and drinking my tea or coffee. They got it in their heads I was a Narc and undercover officer because, as the Constable said, they

126

said or believed, "Wouldn't no white woman live out there in that ole house by herself. White people don't live like that." They thought I was getting evidence on them and that, since I was a woman, they could scare me off. Like I said before, idiots.

I wondered if they really had a clue what lay in store for them if they had hunted me that night. About fifty yards from where I hid was the plastic bottle I practiced shooting at six footers. I was prepared, and intended to protect myself. I had listened to Alex Jones more than enough.

The old Constable warned me and The Postman to be quiet, to just let them continue to watch. They had plans for the old mobile home the cookers had set up. A week or so later, it burned down, under the watchful eye of an old fellow who knew his tracks.

As it turned out, I was never involved in the court proceedings and never heard another word from the court.

~ ~ ~

I was a little shaky about sleeping at night for a while.

The cow owner had long ago built a big bull feeder. It was an overly big trough made out of 2x10's and set down on old creosoted power poles. It was more or less bull-proof. Bulls push each other and jockey for field chunks and salt blocks, so it was seriously strong and deep. It was off to the west, in a grove of pines away from the house. I left the girls in the house. Otherwise, they'd be off hunting all night.

I pulled out my sleeping bags and a quilt, my fanny pack, and the 20-gauge and made me a bed in the trough. It was almost surreal laying there. I wasn't afraid but knew enough to have a healthy, cautious approach to these kind of people. And having survived for a number of years out here alone, safety and survival were my first priority. It wasn't unduly cold, but chilly, and sometime during the night I dozed off.

When morning came, I woke up to the cries of a hawk and the cleanness and pureness of my world. As I turned to get out of my make-shift bed, the does were in the meadow, but they didn't stir. I think they were so used to me moving about area. And I smelled like the woods.

I could tell their tummies were swelling with new fawns. Soon, I would get to see a new generation of nature born to this place. They would be born in the little spiritual spot I so often visited to meditate and pray.

I went back to the house and let the girls out. There was no work this week, so I would work around the place and rest. I put on coffee water and then went out back to start my fires under my water tubs. I filled them from the cistern and looked around. This was my soul place and my love has always been immeasurable for it. Tears always came to my eyes and my heart squeezed a little bit when I thought about it.

How could anyone be so lucky.

I don't know that I was ever in any further danger, but still, I spent a couple of nights out in the feed trough before I finally settled back down and started to relax again. And I never mentioned it again to anyone.

I realized I had let myself get too lax, too comfortable with my surroundings. I had to stop doing that. I hated the thought that I had to be always on-guard again, like I did in the city, but I had no choice. Trouble always moves to where there is the least resistance. Again I thought about Tom Clancy's words – *Trouble Rides a Fast Horse*. His words had become mine and they came to be closer to my life than I ever thought possible.

All week I worked around my house. I raked leaves and hauled wood to the front porch.

I would have some work soon, and life would start to change again.

~ ~ ~

A few days later, The Postman came to tell me I needed to work. I would be the only one now.

He didn't tell me, but when I got to work early the next morning I was stunned. All the new splitters were gone.

I was standing there looking with my mouth open when The Postman came up behind me and said, "He sold them." The Ego had sold all but two of the splitters.

I should have been used to it, the total disregard for his Dad's investment in all the equipment, and the contracts we had left.

I needed to split as much as I could. We needed a dozen pallets in the next couple of days. I did twelve in a day once, but all I got out that day was seven. Thank God The Ego didn't take the older 35-tonner. I needed it for our hickory customers. Splitting full cords of green hickory was hard work on me *and* the splitter.

I took my lunch break and went in to see how The Postman was doing and I didn't like the way he looked. The stress of everything going down the tubes was getting to him. I made a decision to call his son and express my concern.

When I went back out and looked around, I thought back on the years. Where had the time gone? Then it dawned on me how long I had devoted myself to this woodpile business. And I realized I had needed this place as much as it needed me and that I'd enjoyed every year of it.

What a life. Who would have thought it, huh?

~ ~ ~

The Postman's Oldest Son showed up and was livid. He came to my place to ask me if I would check on his Dad as often as I could. His health was declining and this mess was making him sick.

Even still, no one could talk him out of doing whatever he had to for the Youngest Son, who by this time was in his mid-thirties.

By the end of the week, he would sell off the little forklift, the one we sent on the trailer to unload the pallets. We would have to hand-load the bundles onto the trailer because we couldn't load pallets anymore and the customers wouldn't like it. The bundles had to be unloaded by hand and then they would have to figure a way to display their wood and it was all very labor-intensive. Oh dear.

By the end of November, we had lost next year's contracts.

All we had left was our barbecue-wood customers and The Postman's deep debt.

I was heartbroken, but I knew it wasn't my problem. I'd do what I could, but the many times I had waited on my money and the shabby treatment I received from The Ego and Fake Fanny...well, it left a bad taste in my mind.

~ ~ ~

I was sad, of course, and a bit depressed, but it would give me time to work on the mobile home I bought way back when. And then, right on cue, Middle Son showed up.

The back wall needed to have its stud work redone. Lumber was still cheap then. We would strip out the old carpet and rework the wall. I was happy to see it had good copper wiring and good sinks and tub. We cut our studs and other pieces at The Postman's.

My son wanted to cook in the outside kitchen. He said it brought back memories, so we baked chicken on the old grill and baked taters in the coals.

That night, a bad cold front moved in. It froze water in the kitchen. I would receive mail from the lawyers, and a small check. Whew! Sometimes even a blind squirrel finds a pecan.

It was so cold, we had to put off working outside for a couple of days, but we got to spend time together, which I enjoyed because I seldom had family out. It had been a year or so since I had seen son number two. He'd been working out of state.

~ ~ ~

I was driving an old Chevy Malibu. It was a sweet old car, but it wasn't a Road car. The Road was hell on shocks. I needed another truck. And I was up to my ears in paperwork. Every time I had to look at the same paperwork over and over, I felt like I was burying my husband again and again and it wasn't easy. I wished he had never filed the lawsuit. He wasn't the one living with it.

Time would go way too fast now.

That winter for the first time in all the years I had been there, I got sick, very, very sick.

~ ~ ~

Christmas was on me again and work was sporadic. As I had more free time now, I would go visit the kids, even though the thought of heading to Houston, with all its traffic and so many people, always made me nervous.

The Postman and I had become good friends, or as good as two loners could be on The Road. He would always honk when he went by my place and once or twice a month we would go to town together for groceries. But he was going to his older sons' for dinner, so The Road would be lonely. It was a good time for a visit.

As I got ready to go, I heard a honk at the gate. It was my young neighbor, all grown up. It had been years since I'd last seen him and my, how he had filled out. Dog sat between a young lady and him and he was beaming!

When I reached the gate, he hugged me like a long lost parent and then introduced me to the young lady, his bride to be. He still had a year of school to go, but she was a college graduate. She was very shy, but she had such a gentle smile and a quiet loving demeanor towards The Boy. I knew she would be the right person for him.

He wanted to see his dad and my heart sank as his father had fallen deep into drug use and the place was a mess. I asked him if he knew how bad his dad had gotten. He said yes, that he talked to him and could tell. We talked about me being out here alone and I told him how much I missed his visits. He explained to his fiancée that we used to visit and talk and told her about Knight Rider, the fawn we had rescued.

When they were ready to go, I got his new address and told him I expected an invitation to the wedding. His grin was followed by a blush and the 'ahhh shucks' look of his I knew so well.

"Of course," he said.

I had to tear-up after he left. Where had the time gone?

Feeling a little washed out, I thought I'd lay down awhile before I left for Houston. By dark I was running a high fever and couldn't seem to move my muscles.

I took some aspirin but threw it up and decided not to take any more, which was a very good thing as at the time, I had no idea I was dehydrated and would soon be in serious danger of losing kidney function.

I tried to heat some soup, but started shaking and could barely stand. When my vision doubled I knew I needed help, but I also knew I couldn't reach anyone by cell phone without leaving the house and either going to the pasture on the ladder for a signal from the cell service towers or get in the car and go to the end of the road. The way I felt, neither was an option.

I remember heading back to bed with a raging fever. And I kept thinking it must have been the meal I had eaten with the Postman on a shopping trip to town, that maybe I had food poisoning.

131

I lay there for two or three days.

I had long stored gallon of jugs of water by my bed because it was the coolest spot in the house, so I could reach them without moving too far. I remember trying to drink and the girls wanting to go outside to potty, but not too much else. Sammie whined and stayed with me, cuddled up near my face. Tippy lay close watching me. I think they kept me warm as I wasn't able to light the burner. I had quilts piled on the bed.

Then I remember hearing my Youngest Son's voice and riding someplace. And when I came back to my senses, I was in the hospital. I can't remember even now, but I must have gone without eating or drinking for a few days before my son found me.

I do remember being hooked up to bottles hanging from stands. And getting shots. And sleep that seemed troubled. And things I needed to do but couldn't get up and do them, which made me mad. And being mad because they wouldn't give me any salt. It's strange the things our brains choose to remember when we're sick and close to death.

The doctors and nurses all told me I fought them. Sounds like me. My son said I was fighting to get up and that the Spirit of Battle was with me. I was struggling to come back.

I spent a week in the hospital, near death in kidney failure thanks to a virus I must have picked up in town. I had gotten so terribly dehydrated without even knowing it. I hadn't been sick in years. I had been isolated from illness and had no antibodies to fight it.

My kidney function improved and my vitals came back into normal range. To this day, I have a false blood pressure reading. It seems low when in reality can be a little high. And I will still dehydrate easily and have been warned that as I get older, it could get worse.

Years of surviving bitter cold, horrible heat, working in all conditions, and pushing myself to the max hadn't done me in but a virus had, helped by not working and it being cold enough that I hadn't been drinking enough water.

As it turned out, when I hadn't shown up as scheduled my son came to see if I had broken down or what had happened and that's when he found me. Now, he wanted to take me back to town but I begged him to let me stay. It terrified me to think of leaving this place.

There were way too many people at his house and I knew I just couldn't take it. This was my world and I would live with the consequences of staying.

On the way back from the hospital, we stopped by Walmart and bought lots of jugs of water, noodles, cookies, and yes, some sweet rolls. That's when I discovered the shelf-stable milk in quart cartons. It stayed good until you opened it. Once you did, though, you had to refrigerate it like regular milk, so I had to drink the whole quart when I opened one.

He also stocked my porch wood pile and made sure my propane tank was full. He stayed the night and very, very, reluctantly left me there the next morning.

Tippy and Sammie were beside themselves to have me back. With all their whining and jumping up and down, they made me smile.

I decided then that I wouldn't work the woodpile again. I was moving up in years and all the time I put in there had taken its toll and was hurting me now.

There comes a time when you just have to realize your limitations. I had reached mine.

~ ~ ~

I was home and happy, but I was still very weak. I spent hours on my little porch reading and drinking tea and water, and working on my latch-hook rug.

To say the house and fifty acres nursed me back to health sounds so foolish I know, but it did. At first, I just walked around the ole house to build up my strength. I waited for the mail to arrive and when it did, I was so weak it felt like a million miles to the mailbox and back to the house.

My cash was getting low, so I needed to get to my money hidey hole, but it seemed impossible that I could walk that far and back. I decided to go early in the morning while I had the energy.

It was very cold when I got up. After breakfast, I wrapped up and started to the back of the property where my stash was.

Breathing the cold air seemed to clear my head and energize me. When I reached my meditation spot, I saw the does, five of them, with their fawns. I walked gently, like I always did, and they didn't run.

They just watched me with their tails twitching and ears alert as they took turns guarding the fawns that, with their spots, were almost invisible in the dead grasses. That was the most healing thing I have ever experienced. Their trust, their knowing I wasn't a threat, lifted my spirits and energized me.

I moved on toward the back of the fifty acres. As I walked, a white tail hawk flew over-head making her hawk sounds – another sign of life.

On the way back to the house, I sat down to rest in my prayer place. I thought about the years past, the joys and sadness, the struggles and triumphs, and wondered what I would do now. Tears of gratitude, frustration, pride, failure, and joy fell. I don't know how long I sat there, but when I stood to go home, I had a greater strength and a renewed resolve to continue my life on The Fifty.

When I got back to the house, I decided a hot bath in my makeshift sauna was the key to washing away the tired, ill feelings I had so I loaded wood under the water tubs, then baled water ever so slowly until there was enough to start the fires to heat it.

I had been so sick and weak I didn't realize how much time had passed since my first day on The Fifty. I didn't realize I was in the year 2002 until I noticed the date on mail I began receiving from the lawyers. I had begun to hate lawyers, with their endless questions, over and over, about the same thing. And, of course, they charged for every call, letter, and appearance in court on behalf of the lawsuit.

I enjoyed the warm water. By the time I was done, the day was fading fast, but that was okay. I had renewed myself. No – as I healed, the spirit of this place was renewing me and protecting me, as always, and loving my presence on her land and in her house as much as I loved her being there for me.

~ ~ ~

Winter came and seemed to stay forever. In a way, that was good. The cooler it was, the better I felt. Rainy, freezing weather can be fun.

I had wood ready on the front porch and would load up the burner, make my black tea, and read. I read and read and worked on my rug.

There was an article in *Backwoods Home Magazine* that showed how to make rag rugs, so I tried to make one. The result was hilarious. It wasn't a round or oval or square rug. No description fit it. Still, it was my rug I made with my own hands. I used it in my back porch bathroom/sauna.

Early one morning in June, I heard a honk at the gate. It was FedEx with a letter from my lawyer. It had an immediate return sticker on it and he said he'd wait while I read it.

Lo and behold, the lawsuit was finished. The company had settled. I signed the agreement, kept my copy, and the guy took off with it.

As administrator of the estate, I would have to appear in court in August. I needed to make arrangements. So, I got in my old Malibu and went to the end of the road to call my Lawyer. I explained to him that I had been very sick but would try to make the hearing. He said he would take a chance and set up a three-way call with the judge and that I was to call him back.

The lawsuit had dragged on for so long I had doubted I would ever see a dime and mostly didn't care anymore. Lawsuits are not anything like the easy things you see on TV commercials. I had to provide info that I didn't always have. What had started out at 33% of the proceeds turned out to be about 67% after both sets of lawyers got through with their invoicing.

Think twice about it and you will know greater peace just letting it go. I had cussed Jim a million times for it, but he had signed binding contracts and the Estate had to abide by them.

When I called back, I was told the conference call was on for the next day and that I had to call at the time they set up as the judge was not always a happy camper and if I was late or if I missed the call, he might well hold up the decision longer.

I didn't want to trust my cell phone and the spotty reception in our area, so I asked The Postman to use his house phone.

The call with The Judge lasted about 40 minutes. I found him to be very nice and easy to talk to. A probate judge knows these things drag on for years. All I had to do after talking with him was to send my attorney the admission and dismissal forms from the hospital so he could file them with the court.

In July, I received notice that the Judge had accepted my phone conversation as sworn testimony. Wha-hoo!

Please, for your family's sake, write a will. Ever since Jim died, my life had been in the hands of the state. Soon, once his estate was finally settled, I would have full control of my life back again.

I was feeling giddy at the thought, and at the prospect of having some money for a change. The one thing I wanted more than anything was something I had never owned. And I wanted a black one.

The days seemed to drag now that it was over and all I could do was to wait.

I will never forget the day the waiting ended. This time, it was a UPS truck that showed up and honked. I had to sign for a certified letter. Clipped inside was a check and a notice from my lawyer, to call as soon as it arrived.

I watched the truck pull away, then went back into the house and whooped and hollered, danced, laughed, and cried. At long last, it was over with. The heirs received their checks and I had mine. There wasn't much left after the lawyers got theirs, but I would have enough to do something I had dreamed of for years.

My hair was clean so I didn't have to heat water to wash it. I dug out my best jeans and shirt, slid into the old Malibu and went to the bank.

I remember shaking. I was so nervous I could barely sign my name on the check. I asked for some cash. For the first time in years, I didn't have to go to work at the woodpile in the heat and the cold or put up with the attitudes of The Ego, Fake Fanny, or anyone else to survive.

When I was done at the bank, I headed to the GMC dealership in Huntsville. And there she was, waiting for me, in the color I wanted.

Of course, I wasn't about to just pay the sticker price, so the haggling began. It took a while, but in the end, I got what I wanted – my beautiful, black half-ton GMC pickup.

I asked the salesman if we could drive around a bit. I was way too nervous to take off on my own and really couldn't see through the tears – the happy tears.

He took me to a side road and showed me all the bells and whistles. He let me drive and adjusted the air conditioning. Yes, real A/C in a vehicle of mine! I had lived for years in the elements, so this was a whole new experience to me.

The salesman had her washed, because I demanded it, and filled with gas. I had to leave the Malibu there until I could get someone to drive her home.

The black color was unusual. It had a metallic sheen under the paint. Lord how beautiful she was. As I drove home, I was a creeping along like an old lady; scared to death I would wreck it.

I had to run some errands before I could head home, so I went into town to the feed store. I told my friend, the owner, to come see what I got. I told him I bought four new tires and they gave me a truck to go with it. He laughed and told me I would have to wash it often.

Oh, hell! I forgot about the dusty old road. Oh well, I would cross that bridge later.

It was getting late and when I reached the house. I parked her in the shade, by my bedroom window, a spot I thought would be away from the dust.

Wrong.

I took pictures of my new beauty and the ole House together. Then I walked around her and just stood in awe of the first new vehicle in my life.

Awesome!

Tippy and Sammy barked at her. It was something new in the yard and it wasn't leaving.

Tomorrow, I would take her to show The Postman. I was getting very tired. I went to sleep looking at her – my Ebony Baby.

~ ~ ~

The Postman was thrilled. He had wanted me to buy a Nissan, but they were a little out of my price range.

And he looked sideways at me and asked, "Black? Seriously?"

Already my new Baby was dusty.

I went home, got dressed, put Tippy and Sammy in the truck, and started off toward Houston. I had to show the kids my beauty.

Have you ever smelled a new truck? Experienced the first miles ever put on one? I hadn't and I was in awe.

I don't mean to sound like a barefoot, uneducated hillbilly, but this was totally new and for the first time in years, I was experiencing a totally new thing.

My new truck. To the left is the meadow with the hog wallow.

My kids were very happy with me and my new truck. Then the *why don't you move back to town, mama* talk began.

My Youngest Son knew where there was a lot I could buy for back taxes and we went to see it. He talked about me putting the old mobile home on the lot and moving back in or renting it. Renting it didn't even fit in my plans.

But I signed a check for them to approach the tax office with. It would be an investment and it was cheap to say the least.

Then I gathered up the dogs and headed back to the House. I was amazed at how easy the ride was.

When we got to the gate of the ole House, I looked at her and knew I wasn't near ready to leave her. I wondered if I ever would be.

~ ~ ~

I was finally putting on some weight.

For so long, I looked like a pale, skinny scarecrow, but now I was filling out and color had come back to my face.

I had two other trips to make.

138

There was a little church that I had occasion to attend. The former pastor had stripped them of a great deal of money and left the church to rebuild. Before I left the House, I wrote a check.

It was many miles away and I didn't take the girls as it was too hot for them to stay in the truck. The doors were always open for prayer and when I arrived, I was able to sit inside for a bit to pray and meditate before the new Pastor happened to come through the church. It took him awhile to remember me, but when he did, I told him I had a gift for the church.

If you have ever belonged to an orphan church, one left to recover without a Pastor, you know the grief anger and how serious it is for there to be no Shepard to lead. He looked tired and he asked me to move back to the area as they had need for me. I had to decline and handed him the envelope as I thanked him for his prayers.

I was called an idiot for giving money to a church. I was asked how I knew what they would do with the money.

I had to tell people that I didn't know and that it was none of my business. My God had prompted me and that's all I needed to know and obey.

I'm happy to say that church has grown under the new Pastor's guidance. He and his wife spent many hours in prayer and counseling the folks in the congregation who were so distressed by the previous Pastor's actions. They were a hurting church.

~ ~ ~

For so many years, my days were all very much the same, but now, they became something they had never been – kind of dreamy.

I'd be so amazed when I'd look at my new, black beauty. The girls and I would walk The Fifty and while they swam in the pond, I would watch them and the area around me, taking in the quietness and grace of nature.

I bought more water kegs. Bottled water became very available and I stocked up. I was able to afford more plastic to cover the inside of the house. I spent the fall doing that. I mowed, I ate, and I read. I decorated pine cones for my Christmas tree. This would be a different Christmas.

Tippy and Sammy seemed much more at peace. They stayed by my side constantly and seemed more on guard than usual. I think they knew my health had suffered. If humans could only love and be this faithful.

I would sit in my Someday Kitchen and write letters. I read endless articles on questions about living off-grid. Having been off-grid so long, and not having contact with many others, I had to laugh. I wasn't the only one in-love with a simple way of life.

I still am.

~ ~ ~

I gifted each of the kids with a small check for Christmas.

I made plans to have the mobile home moved to the lot so my Middle Son could work on it. She had sat there for so long, when the movers showed up, I was a bit nervous about letting her out of my sight, but she needed work and it couldn't get done here. Although the driver was an expert, we had to take down the gate so he could swing her out. Then he straightened it all up ever so slightly and off they went.

I followed in my truck to make sure she was set up ok, but my Youngest Son saw to it. He'd set up blocks for her, so on the way in, I stopped and bought tie-downs.

Remember all the gutter and siding pieces I had salvaged? The siding became the skirting around the bottom. Every piece of the scavenged material was used.

We used 1x2's for the top hanger and 2x4's for the vertical nail posts.

I felt great when it was all done. Tied down and skirted as the law required, she sat on the lot legally and when I came into town to see the kids, what a mother-in-law house I had!

~ ~ ~

The 2002-2003 winter was unusually cold and I became very conscious and cautious of dehydrating again. I made my skillet cakes, chocolate mostly, and it was cold enough in the kitchen to ice them.

Spring 2003 brought with it the collapse of my Youngest Son and a strange quietness I didn't understand from the kids. My daughter-in-law came to get me, asking for my help to get help for her husband.

You may remember he's an electrician. I knew he had been seriously shocked on a ground wire they were installing. Dampness caused the energy to jump to ground. It took a few days to get his heart stabilized but he seemed to be recovering well. Then he got the news that his oldest brother, my first born, had been arrested.

Youngest Son couldn't believe his hero and buddy was in jail. He collapsed from a nervous breakdown and had to be hospitalized and medicated. He knew he would have to tell me and he couldn't. He didn't understand how it was possible. Neither could the rest of us, but he was a very sensitive and caring man and it affected him deeply.

I almost lost it myself when I heard, but concern about the physical condition of my Youngest kept me from just dropping where I stood. My Middle and Youngest Sons and I were beyond belief, unable to comprehend how it could be. Sometimes, it takes time to wrap your mind around these things. And sometimes, you just can't.

I called The Postman, told him I had the two girls with me, and asked him to check the house because I would be a few days getting back.

Youngest Son finally got out of the hospital and went home. He curled up in bed with his back to us. His world had been shattered, because through all the years he and his brothers were growing up, through all the things that happened, it had been us four, together. But now our circle had been broken. And though we tried hard to remake it, it was too hard with a link gone.

As a Mother, I searched my mind and the past.

Things had been very rough as a single Mother in the 60's and 70's. My feelings of guilt for those years past became as great as my son's depression. My Mother was gone, so I couldn't call her to talk things over. The only thing I knew how to do was continue praying.

I didn't know how to tell anyone what he had done. I still don't. I couldn't bring my mind to it. After spending a week with them, I told them I needed to go home. I needed that desperately.

When I finally arrived back and was trying to unlock and unchain the gate, I couldn't hold it in any longer. The screams came, and I shook with all the energy that anger, grief, and helplessness can bring.

~ ~ ~

In my desperation, I needed to return to the days of old, when I cooked in the backyard, so I built a fire and started to boil water for coffee.

It was one of those cold, cloudy, still days, and I found it calming me, leaving me feeling peaceful. As it grew dark, I sat by the fire drinking the strong brew. Not that I ever had the chance to drink weak coffee. It seemed, no matter how little or how much coffee grounds I put in the pot, it always ended up strong. As I sipped, I wondered if this calm would last, if I would ever again truly have a sense of peace without worry.

Eventually, I moved into the house, lit the lamps, built up the fire in the wood burner, and sat in the chair, my dogs at my feet, warming up, and asking God for direction.

~ ~ ~

I woke in the chair to a cold house and the girls asking to go out, so I wrapped up in a blanket and stepped outside. The cold crisp air instantly sharpened my foggy brain and I knew what I had to do. I had to go north and see to my son. I just had to. He was a grown man, of course, but he was still my child.

I went around back and started my water tubs, then headed back inside to make coffee. As I stood in the Someday Kitchen, I looked out at the meadow. The mist hung and the sun shone through it. I can't describe the sight, but it was mystical and beautiful.

When my water got hot, I made a bath in my back porch sauna and soaked the agony out of me.

~ ~ ~

The Postman was always up early, so I went down to see him. I told him what had happened and he cried. It seemed he and I had the same kinds of problems as time went on.

I hated to ask him if he could see to the girls – Lord how I hated to leave them – but the trip would be long and my truck was a single cab with no room for them on such a long trip. He said yes and I gave him a key asking him to let them out in the morning and put them up at night.

I split open a large sack of dog food and filled every pot I had with water. I put papers down for them, although I knew they'd pop before they pottied in the house.

They knew something was up. As I got ready to leave, the Middle Son showed up. It was always uncanny the way he would show up just when something happened or he was needed. He had heard about his brother and came to see if I was ok. I hugged the girls and told them to take care of the house. Damn I hated leaving them.

He had brought a change of clothes and I asked him if he'd go with me. We'd go out the back way and stop at the Postman's place to let him know.

The Postman had been very concerned about me going by myself. He had even offered to go with me, but he wasn't well enough for the trip.

We went through town and I stopped at the bank to get money for gas and we left for the north.

I have driven all over the country, but this was the longest, most aggravating trip I ever took. We hit rain, we hit sleet, and we hit snow. I had only seen snow a couple of times in my life and had never driven it.

It was a good thing I had read my truck manual.

~ ~ ~

We arrived on a Thursday afternoon. My Son's trial was to be Friday afternoon. That gave me a little time.

His lawyer had been appointed by the court. We had an early Friday appointment to see him. It's something I hope no parent ever has to do. Knowing all the good in your child doesn't make a very good defense. It doesn't matter to the court one bit.

Having been through most everything a parent can go through, for the third time in my life, I felt utterly hopeless. There was nothing I could do. Writing a check wouldn't help and there was nothing I could say in court. No matter what I did, I couldn't save him from prison.

My Son's choice to waive a jury trial and go before a judge saved wear and tear on the family. The judge saw me and asked who I was. At the time, only the prosecutor, my sons, and I were in the courtroom with the judge.

I had to stand up before that man and tell him I was my son's mother. I have been in some tough spots in my life, but this was the worst. I could barely stand. The shame and guilt I felt for my son's crime was enormous. I asked myself what I could have done differently as a single mother abandoned by their father at a young age.

One of the female lawyers took me aside later and told me something I would not understand for years. "You did your best," she said. "As an adult, he made a decision to do this crime."

My child was sentenced to seven years and would do four years of parole once he was released.

Do I condone what he did? No! But I will never hold him solely responsible.

He had a week to get his affairs in order. He was out of jail on a large bond and had many things to take care of.

I would spend a couple of years only hearing from him by letter. This would age me and nearly break the spirit I had gained.

~ ~ ~

I had to return to Texas.

My oldest boy was going to prison and there was nothing I could do about it. His brother and I would share a tearful goodbye with him and as I drove away, I knew it would be a very long time before I saw him again.

I have never taken so long to drive 1400 miles in my life. It was like we were in a state of suspended animation. We must have talked, but I can't tell you about what. All I knew was that the miles passed.

When we finally got to The Road, and to the House, I again felt the peace the old place had always brought me. It would have been nice if Middle Son could have stayed awhile, but he had to get back to his work. He rested a while, and as he got ready to go, the look in his eyes broke my heart again.

The girls were so glad to see me and I was so glad for their comfort.

The house was cold, but after I lit the burner and the oil lamps, I could only drop down in my chair. I was drained, worn-out, and so grieved. How I wished for the woodpile once again. I needed something to work out my grief and anger and the shear frustration of feeling helpless. But I now had to grieve and support my other two sons. They couldn't or wouldn't understand until years later. I think that's what saved my sanity. My boys needed me to be strong even though I didn't want to be. I wanted someone to be strong for me for a change, but it seems I never have had much time for self-pity.

Once again, it was just the ole House and me and the girls.

~ ~ ~

It started raining and we had a hard freeze. All I could do was pace the house, read, and decorate my pine cones until I remembered all my *Backwoods Home* magazines.

I dug out my stationary and envelopes, went through every issue I had, and sent for every free information pamphlet I could find.

I had plenty of wood but would have to figure out another way to get wood for next winter. Once the rain stopped, I took the truck to the back of The Fifty and gathered deadfall. As I worked, I kept hearing a tiny squeaking. Finally, I stopped and listened carefully.

Sound in the woods is different and can fool you. It bounces around and makes it hard to know where it's coming from. I think many folks get lost because of it.

As I eased around in the wet and cold, I found the source – three baby squirrels. The storm had blown a tree over and fallen on their mother, killing her. They were so young, their eyes weren't open yet. And they were cold and very hungry.

Now this was right up my alley. I had raised all manner of critters in the years I had lived in the old house.

Isn't it strange? I thought. *More babies in need of care.* I forgot the wood gathering and bundled them in my sweat jacket.

When I got them back to the House, I put a whole bag of cotton balls in a shoe box. There was a ledge-type shelf on the wall near the Burner and I sat them there, with the lid on, as they were very hungry and I didn't want to take the chance of them somehow climbing out and falling off the shelf.

I had no idea how often a mother squirrel fed her babies, but I knew she hunted food for herself and left them for long periods of time. The girls and I loaded into the truck to go to the feed/hardware store. They had kitten and puppy milk. The babies were too weak to nurse on one of those hard, plastic bottles, but I had an eye-dropper and that would work.

After paying for the milk, I went across the street to the little grocery and bought my comfort food, some cinnamon rolls. The old man who owned the store had cut up some meat for his meat counter and he advertised the bones for 25 cents a pound. I smiled, as they would occupy the girls. Old Tippy was a squirrel hunter so this was going to be interesting. I would have to figure out a pen that would keep the squirrels in and Tippy out, but that was a few days away.

I went home, locked the gate, and into the house we went. With the girls in the kitchen, I warmed the kitten milk in a cup on the burner. The poor babies were warming up but my goodness they were hungry.

I found my eye-dropper and began to gently feed them. I didn't know how much they ate, but it seemed when they were full, they just fell over asleep. I laughed and giggled like a kid. Their little tummies were full and they were warm. I figured I would have to get up at night for feedings, but that wasn't hard. On very cold nights, I almost always got up to bank the Burner.

Tomorrow I would find some bricks and see if heating them some before I went to bed helped keep the babies warm. Every once in a while, I'd think how electricity would be nice so I could use a heating pad, or a blow dryer for my hair.

It was rough at first getting up every night to be sure they were warm. They didn't have a warm momma to curl up around them, so I had to do my best.

I noticed one seemed to have something wrong with its mouth. I thought maybe its jaw was broken in the fall, so I was extra gentle feeding it.

In a few days, I knew they could hear because they would squeak when they heard me. Now that'll make your heart smile. It did, mine, but Tippy wasn't very happy. She had spent years trying to catch her one and now there were three living with her!

~ ~ ~

The babies grew hair and seemed to thrive on the kitten milk. Soon their eyes opened and oh my goodness, that was too cute. But they were also moving around, now. I had air holes in the lid of the box and made some hinges out of duct tape, but I knew they would soon start getting much stronger and start climbing, so a pen had to be my first priority. Fortunately, I had an idea.

The Postman had a pair of Yorkies, so tomorrow I would go down to his place and borrow his little dog kennel. That would give the babies room while keeping them safe from my two hunters, who couldn't understand why they couldn't have the squirrels.

Each time I fed them, I looked for different markings so I could tell them apart. They were playful and seemed to thrive. They would nip at me and run up my arms. The one with the hurt jaw seemed to heal, but his jaw didn't work as well as it should. I had already made up my mind that I would turn them loose as soon as they were ready, whenever that would be.

Those cold winter mornings were the greatest. The frosty mist hung over the meadow and it was like looking at a painting. To this day, I think about the peace and solace of those mornings – such peace that I wondered how folks lived anyplace else.

~ ~ ~

My morning routine had become simple. As I did most days, I got up, added wood to the Burner, made coffee in my Someday Kitchen, and let the girls out into a crisp morning.

After I fed the girls and myself, I fed the babies. They'd begun fighting each other for their turns at the eye dropper, squeaking, and climbing on my arms. Once they were satisfied, I got ready to go down The Road to the Postman's place.

When I told the Postman the reason for my visit, he laughed at me, saying he had raised a squirrel once himself. He was happy to let me use the kennel, but he had something else that would work and it would turn out to be better than I thought.

At one time he had raised quail for meat and had the perfect cage for them. It was framed with wood over hardware cloth. I called it woodpecker wire, but it was like a screen of galvanized wire with about quarter-inch holes. It was sturdy, easy to clean, and even had water bottles like you see for hamsters. I'd scald those out to be safe.

We loaded it in the truck and I headed back home where I unloaded it and thought about how squirrels lived in the woods.

I gathered up some branches and broke off pine knots with seeds. Knowing I would have to turn them loose before long, I needed them to learn independence.

The Postman told me about feeding them. He said to give them corn and pecans and seed mixtures. He also told me the key to the squirrels' survival were the pecans; that when I saw one with just a hole in it, it was because they weren't eating it, they were keeping the front teeth shaved down. Squirrels' front teeth never stop growing, so if they didn't gnaw on hard stuff to keep them short, the teeth would grow so long they wouldn't be able to open their mouths and they'd starve to death.

I left the cage on the front porch and went to find them a log with a hole in it for shelter. They were growing well and were about ready to put in the cage. As soon as we got a good, warm few days, I would put them out. But first, I needed to go to town and buy groceries and while I was there, I would get them some seed mixture to start with.

That afternoon, as I started on the thirty-mile trip to town, it dawned on me that I could move around now if I wanted too. I had the means and the vehicle and no woodpile or other responsibility to tie me down. Isn't it strange how we develop a way of living and it doesn't dawn on us for a while, if ever, that we can do things differently?

I didn't have to rush home because I wasn't riding with anyone else. I didn't have to just get what was on my list and get going. I had time and I looked at lots of different things to eat that didn't need a fridge to keep them from spoiling.

I caught a sale on winter sweats. I went to the sporting goods section and browsed through there looking for anything new that would make life simpler, but there wasn't. But I picked up lamp oil and some more plastic and staples to finish the inside of the house. And then I moved on to the book section.

I was always happy with my off-grid life. Now I was happy, I was mobile, and even more independent.

It was a strange feeling after all these years – total independence.

~ ~ ~

I began to leave the ole House more often. It seems strange to say I didn't really know how to go places, but years of not going anywhere except from the house to the woodpile and back again, with only the occasional shopping trip with The Postman, really had formed my daily ways of doing things.

As I sat one morning it dawned on me that I needed things to fix up the old mobile home. It had really retro bath fixtures that were in excellent shape and the kitchen sink was old fashioned and deep, but the plumbing was all galvanized pipe that would need to be replaced. Plus, it would need new faucets and a water heater. The idea of having a water heater made me laugh.

I made a list and a budget and planned a trip to town to purchase the things I needed. What I forgot was that the old mobile home didn't have any appliances. Of course, neither did the ole House, except for the old propane stove.

I realized I still had a busy life here and that I needed to continue with my work here.

Tomorrow, though, would be interrupted by the Postman with another crisis involving his errant son and daughter-in-law.

~ ~ ~

It seemed like mornings always came so early. I wanted to sleep in, but the house was cold, so I got up and started the water to boil for coffee, then got the wood burner going. I love that part of living off grid – being able to warm myself by my own action. Yes, it required more work than flipping a switch or turning a dial on a thermostat, but when did flipping a switch or turning a dial ever give you a feeling of accomplishment and independence?

I had begun to love the coldness of winters. Summers here were almost unbearable. It seemed nothing would cool you down. The heat made the old, uninsulated house feel like a broiler. But all the plastic I had put up on the ceilings and walls helped to stop the cold north wind…well, most of it.

As the house warmed, I let the girls out and checked on the squirrels. I was pouring a cup of coffee when I heard a honk. I knew without looking it was The Postman.

He told me The Ego and the False Fanny had gotten into a fight the night before. He had driven off, wasted as usual, and gotten in to a wreck. He drove off the road and hit a tree, tearing up yet another truck. Unfortunately, this one was a real workhorse and costly.

The Postman needed me to go with him. He still wasn't well and didn't know if he could drive that far. Now, these folks had no idea how hard it was for me to just to *go* someplace. My trips were planned. I needed to wash myself and hair, but no, The Postman didn't have time.

I threw on some clean sweats and grabbed a cap, called the girls in, shut down the burner, and locked the gate. It felt so funny leaving my truck by itself. I had a serious anxiety attack and was shaking when I got in the Postman's truck.

The Ego and his wife had yet another financial venture going. She had once again borrowed money from her parents to open a little corner grocery outside of Huntsville. It was a money maker but these two could mess up a pile of rocks.

When he stormed off after the fight, The Ego had gone to Bryan and of course he went the back way through some rough county and that's when he had lost control and hit an oak, wrecking the truck. Some passerby had taken him to the emergency room where we were to pick him up.

When we arrived, he was waiting. I asked the Postman if he wanted me to drive, but he said no, that it would make his son mad. I asked him who gave a damn.

And then all hell broke loose.

As the Ego got to the truck, he demanded of his Dad, "What's *she* doing here?" and started spewing crap out of his mouth!

That's when all the years of verbal abuse suddenly came back to me. I had distanced myself from him and his wife. I tried to stay out of all their drama. But I was one of the few folks The Postman had to talk to.

Fury I hadn't known in a long while blew through me like a Texas hurricane. I came out of the truck in full-blown, *pull your heart out through your throat* fury mode. This man was a good two or three inches over six feet, but when I let fly, I was ten feet tall and bullet-proof.

I told him I was sick of his hateful, drugged-up ass, sick of his drinking and partying, and sick of his being the meanest, most evil son-of- a-bitch I had ever known. I reminded him it was me and a handful of Mexicans that kept him in money. I let him know I made myself sick working for his worthless self and his worthless wife. I unleashed a string of very unladylike profanities on him and as I stepped forward to knock him on his butt, he suddenly stopped his tirade and looked at me.

I also told him that he was killing his Dad by spending every dime on drink and drugs and his worthless old lady.

I had been there a long time and when she ran off with our payroll I had done without so we could pay the men. I asked him how many times they had slept while we worked in the cold mornings and the ungodly heat of summer.

I was in such a fury I could see the fear in his eyes. And if I'd had a 22-inch oak butt I would have put an old-fashioned Texas ass-whooping on him.

The Postman sat, stunned. He had tried to shut up his son, but that had never worked. It always ended in a screaming and cussing match between them.

Suddenly the Ego said, "Let's go home," which suited me, before I killed the worthless idiot. I asked the Postman to let me drive and he did. He was so tired and shaken.

When we got to my gate, I got out and the old man gave me a hug before he slid into the driver's seat. He said, "Thanks Hun" with tears in his eyes. Hun. That was his name for me. To this day, I don't ever remember him calling me by my real name.

The Ego had passed out in the back seat.

~ ~ ~

I unlocked the gate, just hanging the chain instead of re-locking it, because I had to go out later for supplies.

As I stepped on the front porch, tears came. The fury of the years had been released in a few moments of anger. They were tears of sheer joy though. I had said what I couldn't say before for so many years.

When I worked the woodpile, I had to take what they handed out. I didn't always keep my mouth shut, but I knew that job was all I had, the only way I could survive.

I muttered, "What now big boy? How you going to pay all your bills? How will you keep up the hateful wifey and lifestyle? I win. By golly I win."

Damn fools.

~ ~ ~

Of course the Ego and The False Fanny made up as they always did, even when she stayed gone for weeks or months. She had been living in the back of the little store.

I wondered if I would ever see her again, and sure enough, one day a few weeks later, I heard a honk at the gate. It was The Fanny.

I stood there in my bring-it-on mode and she was being sugar sweet. My mental alarm went off. She wanted *me* to come to work for her in the store! Talk about stupid.

I looked at her and asked, "Do you really think I would do that? You have treated me hateful and cheated me for years."

I let fly on her. I let her know folks weren't as stupid as she thought they were, they were just desperate for jobs, and that none of us could ever stand her or her ego-ridden husband.

Her fake eyelashes were just fluttered trying to think of a comeback.

"Did it ever dawn on you that you had control over your life?" I asked. "It did me."

I told her she had about five seconds to get in her truck and get the hell off my place.

She did, and in a hurry I might add.

~ ~ ~

Spring wasn't too far off, but it seemed the wind and cold would never quit. But I was at such peace that winter.

I really hadn't thought about moving to an easier life. I was so entrenched in my world. I had lived this way so long, had learned to do so much, and made a home out of impossible circumstances, I didn't know if I would even fit in with other people.

As always, water was what I most worried about. Now, with the truck, I could carry all my jugs to the Feed Store to fill them; all eight of them. That was exercise for me. Eight times fifty or sixty pounds was a lot of weight lifting.

Before I left the house with them, I would add about three tablespoons of Clorox to each using a tiny juice glass I had found and marked the measurement on. Winter wasn't as worrisome, but summers worried me. Water will go stale in the Texas heat and the chlorine stopped that.

I tried parking that black truck every place I could find, including behind trees at the back at the pond until a storm taught me that wasn't exactly the place to put her, trying to keep the gritty dust off her. She would be a couple of years old before I stopped worrying about it and started treating her like a truck.

That winter I discovered something. I had been wanting to bake more bread and try different recipes, but I knew the ole House was too cold for bread to rise and that it would be hard to get it warm enough.

On one of my trips to town, I stopped at a used goods place. I was really looking for Army wool blankets or quilts. You can never have enough warm stuff. Never.

As I browsed, I saw an old metal bread box. Bingo! I had an idea. If I put two bricks on top of the Burner, I could set the breadbox on it with the dough in a covered bowl inside and let it sit there long enough for the dough to double itself. The bricks and the air space they made kept it from getting too hot

It worked like a charm and if the embers in the Burner were dying down, it worked even better. I was so proud of myself.

Rye bread was a flop. Even the dogs wouldn't touch it except that Tippy saw fit to bury it. That was funny.

The wheat bread was a little heavy, but tasted good. But my yeast rolls – oh my goodness – became a favorite to bake.

The squirrels were growing and it was getting close to the point of releasing them. They had long since started eating on their own.

I knew I would have a hard time letting them go, but I did, making sure there was plenty of corn and when I could find them, pecans, in case they couldn't find food in the woods.

I kept the one with the broken jaw. It had lived, but it wouldn't be able to survive on its own. I named it Trinity. Trinity the Tree Rat would live to be almost 3 years old, about the normal life span. They just wear out their bodies. But he wouldn't die here.

On the dreary wet days, the girls stayed close to the house. I would bundle up and walk The Fifty. I loved the misty cold. It cleared my brain and I would get to see the deer.

Rabbits were really getting thick. The year before the Parks and Wildlife had a coyote kill-off and the rabbits were reproducing again.

The hawk was building her new nest.

The beauty of winter walks in Texas is that the snakes are all in a hole or someplace hibernating. I could walk without having to watch my every step.

With it so cold, I could leave my cooler on the back porch and the ice kept much longer. I had bacon and stew meat in it. That day's meal would be stew and cornbread. And I would make a skillet cake.

One day when I returned to the house, the mail had arrived and I had an invitation to a wedding. My first born grandchild was getting married. Now this presented a real life problem – clothes.

Good grief, a real *girl* problem!

~ ~ ~

I was concerned for the Postman's health. I would go clean for him, as usual, so it was easy to see things weren't right with him. He seemed to sit and watch reruns of Nascar all day, snacking and not really eating. He tried to keep things going but he seemed so fragile.

One day, as usual, I heard the honk at the gate. I always thought of folks honking as ringing my door-bell.

It was The Postman. He said the man who bought hickory from him needed a trailer-load for his BARBQ place. He was one of his biggest individual customers. He always paid cash for the wood and paid me cash to split it.

Damn! I would do anything to help my friend, but to feed his worthless hangers-on stuck in my throat. And I didn't want to push my health. I still had days when I wasn't feeling well and just drifted through my chores. And I wondered where we would get the wood. He told me a logger friend of his was bringing it from some acreage he was logging.

Good Lord. I agonized over it for some minutes before I told him okay, but his bunch had better stay out of my face. I knew he needed the money. I did also and if it had been anyone else, I'd have said no. But this was The Postman. This was one of those times when my principles were overridden by my caring and concern for this old friend.

I asked when the man would be delivering the wood. He said tomorrow and I told him okay. As luck would have it, the logger sent a man to cut the hickory into butts for me, so I would not handle the chain saw. The Stihls weren't too bad but the Huskys were monsters and to this very day I am terrified of them.

I had always told my men, that logs could kill them and it didn't make any difference if they were being hauled on a fork lift or standing in the woods, and that the chainsaws could be just as deadly in the hands of unskilled hands.

As I walked back to the house after he left, a sadness crept up on me. I missed my job but I had promised myself I would never go back. But a friend needed me and he had always been there for me.

I couldn't let him down.

~ ~ ~

Going into the house, I could see dark clouds building up on the horizon. Well at least it would be cool, I thought. Silly me. It was a blue norther. *(A Texasism meaning a rapidly moving cold front that causes temperatures to fall quickly, is often accompanied by precipitation, and is followed by a period of blue skies and cold weather –Ed..)*

While I was getting ready to go the next morning, ole Tippy looked at me. It was if she knew what I was feeling. We had been together for so long now she seemed to know my every move and what I was going to do.

How I loved those dogs.

It had been a while since I sat down at a splitter, but old training dies hard. The Postman had marked off cords for me by hammering some rods in the ground.

Have you ever handled 24" green hickory? It's the heaviest wood there is. But my muscles remembered and in about 30 minutes I was in sync with my splitter and my wood. And hickory smells so good!

155

It brought back long-ago memories of my sweet rolls and Vienna sausage days; of agonizing weariness, bitter cold and sweltering heat; of dirt and mud and exhaust fumes from all the splitters that seemed to always hang in the air. As I split the wood that day, I was amazed how far I had come.

The man who bought the hickory had his wife with him. She was a sweet, hard working woman.

It took me about two hours for the first cord. I had to smile and thought, *My goodness! You're slowing down old girl.*

Preparation usually took a few minutes. I had to stack the butts alongside me, so all I had to do was roll them off onto my splitter. My muscles ached a bit, but I was ok, though I did keep reminding my body not to quit on me, to hang with me a little longer.

At one point, I looked up and saw the Lady was smiling at me but had tears running down her face. I didn't understand why, but that was okay because she and I both knew women could survive the odds. She had worked alongside her hubby for years to build a huge business. And she knew about survival.

I loved that.

There wasn't anything false about this woman. I had admired her often, when she came with her man to help him, it always made me feel a little sad not having my hubby with me. But then, I wouldn't have learned a thing in all these years.

Some hours later, I finished up my cords, cleaned around the splitter, and folded it down to be moved back into the barn.

It would be the last time.

With great sadness, I looked around one last time, smiled, and muttered, "Whipped that one didn't we?"

~ ~ ~

My plan for the trip to the wedding was simple. Since it was so close to the lot we had the mobile home moved to, I might as well bring the pipes and the bath and kitchen faucets I'd bought. I was able to get Middle Son to measure how much pipe we'd need and make a list of the connections and other hardware. Thankfully, the wiring had all been in fine shape. Copper wiring is the safest you can have. And the folks who built the mobile home did it right. They left slack in the wires so when it was moved, the wires could stretch rather than snap apart.

I'll say this – it was easier buying all the supplies than it was picking out something to wear to a wedding for heaven's sake. Once you have been in survival mode, doing the chores you need to do to stay alive, it's hard to think in other ways.

I had my hair trimmed a bit and bought an understated pant suit that was perfect for after-five. It was off-white and the pants legs flared as was the style of evening wear at the time.

So I had a plan, and I could take the girls with me.

I supplied the squirrel with his pecans, already busted up, cracked corn and his water bottle. Of course I asked the Postman, if and when he came by, to stop and check Trinity's water bottle.

The girls and I took off for the big city. How I hated the exhaust smells and the traffic. I was so spoiled after living a clean, quiet life for so long.

I loved my grandson so much. He was very handsome, and his bride and the wedding were beautiful. The food was delicious, there was music and dancing, and everyone seemed to have a great time. But never in my life was I so glad for anything to be over.

~ ~ ~

Spring was on me. Another year gone by. It seemed impossible that I was already into 2004. Where had the time gone?

Though time passed, I did the same things I always did, including hauling water out of my cistern and building fires to heat it.

In the summer, my solar shower worked so well, I didn't have to waste any water that way. And conserving water was important because we stood in danger of a drought at any time.

Being hot and sweating in the woods is no fun. Dust sticks to you and it feels like the fat has oozed out of your body. It would be a hundred degrees in the ole House during the day.

Imagine, if you can, a tin roof with nothing between it and you but home-milled boards. Having the plastic covering the ceiling and walls helped keep the dirt and critters out of my bed, but the ole House couldn't draw air naturally. Still, it sure beat having scorpions and spiders sleeping with me.

Some years before, my son built me a screen door for the back door. I had gotten braver and would latch it and leave the wooden door open to create a draft through the house. It helped. A little.

~ ~ ~

Over the course of the past few years, I had learned about the Internet and how to get online when I went into town. Then I found the *Backwoods Home* website.

I was in hog heaven. So much information! All I had ever read was in the magazines I bought. And there was a Forum where I could read what other self-reliant people had to say about all sorts of things.

My daughter-in-law got a new HP computer and taught me how to use it to get online when I was visiting. That was easy. But the *Backwoods Home Forum* was a different thing. Not only didn't I know how to post anything, I didn't even know what to do to get on it, so she helped me register for it. While I waited for my registration to be accepted, I read what other people were writing about. Wow! I was so thrilled.

I noticed almost nobody used their own name; that everybody had names that described how they felt, where they were from, what they did, or what kind of hobby they had. I had to choose a name. I considered a few, like Axe Annie and Coastrunner, but I settled on TxAnne.

That Forum was an adventure of its own. At first, I posted on the wrong threads about the wrong things. I seriously got flamed for that, though I didn't know that's what it was called until later.

Fortunately for me, I soon "met" someone online who lived a life many only dreamed about. He was a trapper and longbow hunter, a true survivalist. He had hiked the whole Appalachian Trail and many of the trails and mountains in Maine with his longbow to hunt with and a small tarp for shelter. His Forum name was Melonghunter.

Melonghunter explained how to post and comment on other people's posts. Each subject had a place and soon, nobody was getting upset with me anymore.

He and his wife Terry became dear friends. I'm sad to say that he developed brain cancer and died a few years ago. Part of my world died then. Terry called me his other wife because she knew it was a special friendship we shared. She's a lady of true class.

I met others – a lady called Bama Suzy, Nancy, Kim, MyYellowRose, Gwynyvyr, MnMom, pinetree, and many, many more. Many of them remain friends today, including some guys like tufhelp, offgridbob, heshrugged, AlchemyAcres, and some who have since left us.

I got to know folks from many places. I was always sad when I went back to the ole House and didn't get to talk to them much. But I loved my House more at that time so it was easier to do.

That spring I planted in containers. I had good luck with squash, a few bell peppers, and grew so many pinto beans I had to make me a dryer for them.

I can't say why, since the kids were okay, I was feeling okay, and my girls were okay, but I began to experience an odd sense of foreboding. I felt it, but since nothing was wrong, I paid it no mind.

I became the owner of two yellow tomcats someone dropped off. They would put an end to my rat and mouse problem and they really liked taking on a snake. The two were always together, and they loved to sleep with me.

As spring continued to warm, I couldn't know I had spent my last winter, a season I loved, in the ole House.

And I couldn't know the sheer force of will it would soon take for me not to take my own life.

~ ~ ~

One day, I heard a honk at the gate. It was the Fake Fanny. She said she was there to beg me to come back to the woodpile. They were sorry about how they treated me for so long.

You know that feeling when you think you're in *The Twilight Zone*?

She said The Ego had told her to suck it up and do whatever it took to convince me to come back. All I could do was shake my head and walk off. And as I did, she was still talking. Some people never learn.

Spring is fickle in Texas, with warm days and cold nights. A storm blew up and it was dark and very cold and rainy. It was my kind of weather, the kind that's perfect for Burner time. I had books I needed to read.

That evening the sky turned a strange color. The wind began to swirl and I realized it was a tornado! I grabbed my purse and flashlight and dragged a case of water to the main load bearing part of the ole house, a corner in the west side bedroom. I called the girls to me and grabbed a quilt and pillow. We hunkered down beside the old chest that I had dragged into the ole House so long ago and waited.

Suddenly there was silence and then the roar as the air was literally sucked out of the house. The girls whined and I prayed that Almighty God would turn this monster from us. Curled up in a ball with the girls tucked into my chest, I heard the ripping of trees and a horrible sound like a runaway train with its brakes screeching. It seemed like hours, but it was only seconds, and then it was gone.

I waited for a bit, then got up to see if my truck was still there. I had parked it on the east side. *Lord please*, I kept thinking until I turned the corner and there she sat, covered in leaves, but okay.

You remember me talking about the huge bull feeder that was off to the west of the house? It had been thrown around like a toy, totally ripped to pieces. But all the huge oaks still stood, though some had limbs ripped off. The slash pines weren't as lucky. Many of them were down.

I called for the Tomcats and they came out from under the house. And Trinity the Tree Rat was just fine.

The storm funnel had passed right down the west side of the ole house. Some tin was loose on that side of the roof, but otherwise, the roof was ok. The only damage to the house was that my stove pipe was gone, but that was a small problem and I heaved a sigh of relief.

Then I started laughing, shaking, and crying. We had done it again – survived. It had become a way of life.

After I got my tubs set back up, I realized that if they had not been full of water, they would have ended up a few counties away.

Later that day, after I got my legs to quit shaking, I backed-up my truck and put the ladder on it so I could repair my stove pipe.

The one thing I wished the storm would have pulled down – a red wasp nest – the storm left alone. I didn't mind, though. It was just one more thing life used to test me and some of the tests were quite funny.

~ ~ ~

I had a letter from my daughter telling me my granddaughters and young grandson wanted to come see me and spend a couple of weeks with me.

Oh my goodness! The girls would freak out at the ole House at night with no television, running water, light switches, or a proper bathroom set up.

I'd have to think what to do.

I was doing my regular chores when an idea hit me. I got in the truck and went to The Postman's. I told what I needed and why and asked him about the ole house in back of his place.

He said I could rent it for $25.00 a week which would pay for the electric and water usage, so I drove back to the back and looked at it.

Dam what a mess The Ego's friends had left. But it did have an old TV that worked and a fairly nice bathroom where I could see the kids bathed and properly cared for. We could split our time between houses. But I'd have to do some serious cleaning.

I used The Postman's phone to call my daughter. The kiddos would arrive next weekend. That would give me time to make bedding arrangements and buy food for the young'uns. (Thank God they were mac & cheese eaters!) And I could use the little freezer at the Postman's to store some ice cream and other things.

I walked around outside and there sat an old washing machine. I asked the Postman who said it did work. One more problem solved – laundry for the kids. And there on the side of the old house was a huge sauna tub, which gave me another idea. It would make a small swimming pool for the kids! There were dishes there, but I would have to bring things like bedding and towels down from my ole House to this one.

I went to town to buy some kid stuff – chips, sodas, coloring books, and a Backstreet Boys CD for my soul-mate granddaughter. How she loved that group.

I had told their mother to bring my grandson's trucks so he could play in the sand with them. And for heaven's sake don't send them with any good clothes. Strictly old play clothes.

Getting ready for the kids made for a busy week. It was still cool at night, but that would change quickly. They were due the first week of June.

~ ~ ~

The Postman's rental house had been hit by a tornado, so it was only livable on the bottom floor. I brought in a water hose and scrubbed her down. Then I fixed the screen doors so I could leave the wooden front and rear doors open for fresh air and coolness. There were no beds, so I decided to make pallets for us on the floor.

The old sauna got a good scrubbing before I dragged it up to the end of the steps. For two weeks it would be a play place.

When they arrived at the rental house, we did all the usual hugging and glad-to-see-yas. Their mother, my only Daughter, was going to take off for a two-week-long mother's-day-out and boy, did she need it.

First, her father-in-law had been seriously ill and in a nursing home. Then her mother-in-law had fallen and broken a hip, so she was up to her ears in sick people and her husband's siblings weren't helping at all.

I asked them if they wanted to go see Gmaw's house (that's what they call me) and they all said, "Yes!" I thought it was funny that, as we went down the old dusty road, they were visibly nervous. My beloved soul-mate-granddaughter Heather asked me, "Gmaw aren't you afraid out here by yourself?"

I had to think for a second before I told her, "No baby, not now. But at first I was."

We got to the ole House and I unlocked the gate. Of course, the girls were glad to see them. They loved kids. Sammy took to Katie immediately. That was highly unusual for her. I was Sammy's baby and she seldom had anything to do with other people. Maybe she sensed the connection between Katie and me.

The next two weeks went by slowly; the long days filled with fun. There was so much to do and show them and when we were at my ole House and at The Postman's place, the kids stayed wet for hours in the sauna-pool, playing like puppies and jumping off the steps into it.

162

I would take them to the little store and get ice cream and took them over to the feed store. As it happened, the baby ducks and chicks were in. They loved that.

Grandkids Chris, Heather, and Katie, holding Bear, in the meadow.

A few days before they were to go home, I took them to the back of The Fifty. I took my shotgun, and told them, if we come upon hogs, not to run; just stand still and stay behind me. As we got deeper into The Fifty, up jumped an older buck and four does. He scared the bejeebers out of the bunch. They screamed and I had three kids trying to hang on to me. I laughed until I cried.

They looked at me and my granddaughter put her hands on her hips and looked at me with those blue eyes and said, "Gmaw that wasn't funny!"

Yes it was.

There were wildflowers blooming in the meadow I had looked out to over the years and I got some beautiful pictures of the kids with them. We fished the pond for a while and then hung around the ole House. When it was near time for supper I packed the kids and the girls in the truck and off we went back down to the Postman's house.

Crossing the two wooden bridges, Heather grabbed my arm. "Gmaw, don't cross these old bridges by yourself," she told me. She was afraid of them.

I didn't tell her about the all the times I crossed them when the creeks were swollen or the times they had floated off their moorings.

As we rounded the last curve, there *he* stood – The Big Black Bull. The kids screamed again!

It was springtime and he was jumping and tearing down fences to do his duty, regardless of who did or didn't need his services. And this old bull was of an *I ain't moving* nature. If he didn't want to move, there was no way I could make him.

Most of the bulls out here were polled, but a 1200-1400 pound bull slinging his head was still very dangerous.

I began to inch forward, trying to move him. More screaming. He slung his head and backed up, pawing at the ground, but I gently pushed him and then gave a long honk on the horn. More screaming, but that moved him.

Fun the country way. The old sauna made a great pool. The kids stayed in it as much as they could.

It was usually cool at night and we hooked up my boom box and played the CD of the Backstreet Boys. The kids made up dances, with Heather in charge, of course, as the big sister. I'll admit, I danced with them, there deep in the woods, and we all had fun.

What freedom!

Fed and so tired from the day's doings, they crashed peacefully each night.

During the day, when I took them to The Fifty, they peeked around in the ole House like they expected a monster to jump out. And then it dawned on me – that was the exact same feelings I had in the beginning, out here alone.

One of the nights we stayed until dark so I could light the oil lamps. I even started a fire in the Burner to show them how I stayed warm. I had already made fires under the water tubs and let them each draw water from the cistern. That they found that fascinating. Imagine! Water from the ground!

All too soon, their time with me came to an end and they went home.

One day, years later, when we were talking about my time off-grid with some folks, my oldest grandson would look at someone and say, "She ain't your garden-variety type grandma."

That was the greatest compliment I ever received.

~ ~ ~

I had to pack up the things I had taken to the Postman's house and get them back to my ole House. It was getting really hot much earlier than usual.

Tomorrow I would get my house cleaned up. The dust never quit blowing off that caliche dirt road. My bed would be full of it. I loved the old railroad cabinet for that reason. I could keep my dishes out of the dust.

I had learned a trick from the Mexican men. They would sprinkle water on the dirt in the barn before raking it. It held the dust down for the moment.

I had an old-fashioned sprinkle cap you used to iron with by sprinkling your clothes when you starched them, and I would sprinkle the floors with water then sweep. Worked wonders when you lived in a house where the floors were home milled and rough, although some places were worn smooth by years of walking on them. The Someday Kitchen had an old linoleum floor covering so I could mop it after a heavy duty sweeping. I didn't get crazy, though, about the sandy dust me and the girls tracked in. If I did, I would have worked and worried myself to death.

July hit us that summer with a combination of unbelievable heat and rains. The cistern was full. My rain barrels were full. And I was known to stand out in the rain to cool off. I truly believe the people who saw me thought I was nuts! But they didn't live in an oven.

When the rain let up, I needed to mow. If I didn't stay on top of it, the Bahia grass would get away from me quickly, so I cranked up the old mower and got after it. When mowing, I had to watch for snakes. They like to lie in the tall new grass waiting on bugs and mice.

I was so intent on my mowing I almost didn't hear the truck honking at the gate. I didn't recognize the truck so I went over slowly, not knowing who this was.

Remembering it today, I wish I could make time stand still. I wanted to go back to 1995. I wanted to beg. I cried and I knew that my life as I knew it was over.

The owner was going to do something else with the property.

I had been given a week's notice to move.

~ ~ ~

I couldn't understand why he would do this. Did he want more money? Couldn't I extend my lease a little longer? I didn't know how to live any place else.

Where would I go?

My mind was in a time warp. I was totally stunned, unable to move. I couldn't think. My mind and heart were screaming but I couldn't function.

I know I looked at the man and asked him if he could give me a little longer. Ten years of my life was here. I couldn't even dream of moving in a week.

I left the mower where she sat, went in and made coffee, took a cup to the old porch, and sat down in the rocker. I had to make myself breathe. I couldn't catch my breath and my chest hurt seriously bad. I thought if I had died right there, at least I would have lived my life the way I wanted to.

I sat there for hours as the light faded; sat there into the night. When I finally went into the ole House and lit my lamps, I stood looking at those old beautiful, dear walls, listening to sounds, breathing in the smells. I didn't know how I could leave here. I just didn't understand how to do it.

My little pistol lay there on the old plastic end table I had found at a garage sale. I thought I knew what I had to do. I couldn't move from here. I had made a home in an old house that had been abandoned by the family of the owner.

There was no place that beckoned me. No place else I wanted to be. I had thought I would live out my years here. I sat there with the gun trying to think and not knowing how to even begin to make plans. My God, didn't they understand? No of course not. It was foolish of me to even think they would or could.

I felt a movement at my feet. It was Samantha, old Sammie. She nudged my feet and whimpered. She saved my life that night so many years ago.

~ ~ ~

I had to remind myself about all the years I didn't give up and all I'd been through – almost starving to death; fighting the elements to make a home and a living; doing what I had to do to survive.

I picked up Sammie and she snuggled close as I cried for hours, thinking, trying to figure out what to do.

Sometime the next morning I stood up, went out to the rain barrel, and for the first time ever, I washed my face in it. Determination set in. I wouldn't let this whip me.

I had been watching my money so close and had enough for the trailer I needed, so I went over to a little town near Huntsville and bought a low boy.

I couldn't make myself go to the back of The Fifty, to my special spot. It was impossible. I knew I would lose my sanity for sure if I had to face the beautiful little place I spent so many years in, praying, thinking, and planning.

I confined myself to the area with the things I had to move – the house and the yard. I knew I would save myself great amount of grief if I just didn't look out of that area, especially not at the meadow. I loaded the girls into the truck and headed to my Youngest Son's house.

We don't always understand the reasons we do things or obey a prompting by our Spiritual guide, mine being God. Now I knew. I would move into the old mobile home. I had wondered for a long time what to do with her.

The kids had been after me for years to come back into town. They knew I wasn't a crybaby, but as I told them what happened, that was all I could do. The one thing my daughter-in-law said was, "Well now you can get a computer and get online." And that one thought gave me a reason to be able to move.

I would only bring a few things back into town. I left the old stove. It wouldn't fit in my mobile home and was way too heavy to even think about moving.

I brought my bed, the old railroad cabinet, my enamel table, and burner. I took all the gutter I had, my water tubs, my boot scraper-outside stove, the concrete blocks, the rain barrels, my tools, my axe and hatchets, my potted plants, some porch chairs, and the household goods.

I left the old rocker. I couldn't bear to look at her after all the hours I had spent in her.

It took me three days to pack, load, and get ready to go.

Then I remembered my mailbox. I found my sledge hammer and went out and knocked it off its post.

I still have it.

I went out to the old cistern and drew out a bucket of water. How many of these had I drawn? How much stronger had that had made me?

I took a drink from it, then emptied the rest and untied the bucket, which made me laugh. *Always tie off your bucket.*

I left the outside kitchen and the watershed as they were.

As I came back around the house to put the things on the trailer, I noticed new green growth on the old chinaberry tree I had had cut down.

Well you can push the ole House down now I thought.

You win.

~ ~ ~

I nailed all the windows shut, barred the back door, and locked the outside hasp lock on the front door. And when I pulled out, I chained and locked the gate. But I had to stop. I couldn't breathe. I felt totally lost.

I thought of the two girls, Sammy and Tippy. They knew no other life but the freedom to be themselves. Now I would have to watch them closely. The poor babies. Tippy paced in the seat, whining.

She knew.

Our life of freedom was over.

At that moment, I knew it was up to me once again. I had never been so mentally tired, so spent. I looked back at the ole House. I had never known a house with so much personality and haven't met one since. At that moment, she looked crushed.

My mind reached back to the beginning of my adventure.

~ ~ ~

I remembered the cold, cold nights. And my first ever experience with a wood burner.

I thought about my luck at going to work at the woodpile, where I would have all the hardwood scraps I would need to keep the old house warm; learning how to make the old tin burner draw air and how to shut her down. And being able to make enough money to eat, buy lamp oil, critter food, and the few necessities I needed to live.

I remembered snakes in the house, rats in the house, the ever-present scorpions, and dust in everything.

There were the baths on the back porch, with the solar shower in the summer and the old tub in the winter. And cooking in my outdoor kitchen for such a long time – my goodness was *that* ever a test, as was washing dishes outside – summer *and* winter.

But it was a learning experience. And food has never ever tasted as good.

I will *always* remember smelling like smoke – *Eau de Oak* I called it.

I could never forget all the animals I lived with. Their lives were so intertwined into mine, hanging with me in the awful heat of summer and through some really cold winters, never asking for anything in return but to be with me. Trinity the Tree Rat went with us to our new home. He lived to be three years old.

I remembered all the folks in the small town – a lady at the bank; my feed store friend who, through the years, gave me so much practical advice and supplied me with critter food, pipe for my stove, water buckets, #3 wash tubs, and all the ammo I could buy on 9/11. And the two-pump gas station that doubled as a convenience store, where I bought so many sweet rolls to live on. I think they thought I was a little touched in the head.

I think, at the time, maybe I was.

~ ~ ~

I didn't think I could cry anymore, but I did.

When I arrived at the mobile home, strangely, the newness of being back in a town really took my mind off it a great deal, except at night, when the memories would creep back in. All I could hear were the cars and trucks running down the road half-a-block from us. And all I could smell were their exhaust fumes. I immediately got a sinus headache.

I didn't have a lock on the door on the back part of the old mobile home so I put my box spring up that night to block it. I already had the collars and leads I needed for the girls when I brought them into town, but rarely did I have trouble keeping Sammie close. On the other hand, Tippy was the lead hunter, and she would tear off in a flash if I wasn't careful.

~ ~ ~

I woke up that first morning with my face so swollen from weeping I could barely open my eyes. But I did, and lay there taking stock of my new situation.

I had a roof over my head and indoor plumbing, but no stove and no refrigerator. The thought made me laugh. Thank God I had been doing this for a while. I had my old ice chest and had brought water with me.

It was almost funny. I had forgotten I would have running water in the mobile home. I felt like a cow looking at a new gate, and had to have a talk with myself.

After so many years, I had running water and not just cold! I ran the water until it was hot enough, found the small jar of instant coffee I bought, and made a cup of that foul stuff. Yuck. But I didn't have to dodge any grounds in the bottom of the cup.

I looked around and realized I was back to square one, but I was so tired I didn't care.

~ ~ ~

That attitude lasted all of a few hours. I had lived in survival mode for so long, it just kicked back in. Enough of the self-pity, I told myself. I had to make a home for the girls and myself. Sure, we'd been mule-kicked, and it would take some doing to right our lives, but we'd struggled before.

I got that giddy feeling, the one you get when you're faced with a challenge you know you can win. Ok, I'd grieve and cry and be mad, but I had something to work toward. It wasn't my dream, but it was a place to begin. So I began.

Doors! I needed doors. And I would soon need a roof. It seemed funny to have to be thinking about them, but it sure beat worrying about scorpions.

~ ~ ~

Sometime during the night I woke to the sound of water running. It was raining very hard, the first real rain since I moved in. I lay there for a bit listening and suddenly it dawned on me – the sound was coming from inside the house.

I jumped up and looked in the bathroom but everything looked right there, so I went toward the kitchen and there it was. It looked like a waterfall. One spot of the flat roof had caved in. I grabbed a broom, opened the back door, and swept water for what seemed like hours.

When the rain stopped, I got my Youngest Son to come look at it. I had an idea but needed help.

We went outside where I got an old car jack and asked him to saw a 4x4 across at about 4 feet. We took it and another 6-footer inside.

It took both of us and a ladder to get the 6-foot piece standing upright on the jack, with the 4-foot piece laying across it on top. My son held it in place while I worked the jack until we got the ceiling raised enough to peak and drain water.

~ ~ ~

We realized that moving the old mobile home after it sat in one spot for so long had really warped it, which is what caused the weak spot. Another problem.

For a couple of weeks we held our breaths. I would have to re-jack the jack every so often in the day time and if it rained, I would get up during the night to check it.

My sons studied the old roof and the walls that held it up. The side walls had 2x4 studs with new ones on the north side.

I had to take a serious look at my money.

We planned and re-planned until we were all satisfied we had one that would work and would not leave me broke.

My Youngest Son took the materials list, the low-boy, and my money and drove to a surplus warehouse on old Highway 90.

Thankfully, when my church heard of my problem, they took up a collection to help.

~ ~ ~

We had decided to build a peaked roof. We used 2x6s for the ridge and framed with 2x4s. One of the most expensive parts was the metal hurricane straps, but it turned out to be money very well-spent. They saved my roof when Hurricane Rita hit shortly after we finished rebuilding it.

We covered the roof with tin. I loved it. I could still hear the sound of raindrops on roof of the old House in my sleep.

I really loved the sound.

~ ~ ~

As the morning sun began to warm up everything, I realized the girls and I would soon need to cool down a bit. I needed fans so I got ready for the seventeen-mile drive to town. I had a hot bath, put on some clean clothes, and set off on a new beginning.

As I pulled out of the driveway, I looked over at a four-plex apartment across the street. There were doors leaning up against the side of it. One was a cottage type door and the others solid exterior doors. I'd see if my Son knew who they belonged to.

When I got to town, Walmart to be exact, I was kinda in a stunned mode. For the first time in forever, I didn't need duct tape, staples, or plastic!

Across from hardware, where I picked up light bulbs, was the housewares department, where an automatic coffee pot caught my eye. I would need filters for it. I also found a one-burner electric hot plate. Then I bought a few groceries and headed for the checkout.

By the time I got home, I needed some real coffee. Instant just isn't my bag. I took the new pot out of the box and washed it using water coming out of a faucet. How strange it seemed, after so many years of using the washing tubs outside. Sometimes…many times, I would forget I had these conveniences. I would be trying to figure out what to do about something and then it would dawn on me to just flip a switch. Made me feel like a dummy now and then.

As I waited on my coffee, I made a list. After a bit, I noted there was no coffee and thought, geezzz, it's brand new and it's broken. I started looking to see what was wrong with the new pot when a giggle hit me.

Ya gotta plug it in.

~ ~ ~

My Youngest Son and my Daughter-in-law came by. We sat outside on the tail gate of the truck and had coffee. He told me who owned the doors and I told him what I wanted to do. It was pleasant to have company, but it was very strange to be discussing my plans with anyone.

I needed calm and a feeling of permanency, so set about cleaning and putting things away. I had a spot where I could put the old railroad cabinet and needed to unpack my meager belongings.

I had closets! My clothes could be hung up! In the big bedroom (which wasn't really so big), there was a built in chest of drawers I had forgotten about. And there was a place for towels in the bathroom.

That wasn't so bad. It had been over a decade since I'd had that much built-in storage space.

When fall came, I would smell oak smoke as others cleaned and burned downed limbs and I would fall into a deep nostalgic place. But the new survival sense I gained from ten years off-grid kicked in. I would find as much happiness as I could on this lot until I located a new fifty-acre piece of ground to put this old mobile home on.

That was my new dream – a new place to begin again.

~ ~ ~

I was getting used to all the traffic and noise and wasn't nearly as skittish about it as I was in the beginning. I guess after The Fifty, anything was easy to adapt to.

I talked to the owner of the doors and got them for $5.00 a piece! That was a good sign. Middle Son would install them for me. I loved that cottage door. I wanted it for the kitchen door, so I could sit at my table and look out.

As usual things didn't go as planned. We wound up having to tear out and replace the door frame and studs. The old paneling had to be replaced, too, thanks to weather damage from open windows and a tiny roof leak that I didn't know about at the time. It would come back to haunt me later.

One Saturday morning, my Youngest Son came by. He had found a salvage yard that had paneling for $6.00 a sheet, but you couldn't dig through it and very few sheets matched in the grain anyway. That wasn't a problem, for me, though. I was going to paint them anyway. We hooked up the lowboy and off we went to buy them.

I got enough paneling for the hall, living room, and part of the kitchen. Of course, when we took the old paneling off, we discovered the insulation was past its useful life. The bad insulation was mostly a north wall, which in my area wasn't a big problem, but the south and west sides would be when sun hit in the summer. I had to find some I could afford.

It was a slow process. I could do a lot of work myself, but the boys didn't think I knew a thing, as boys tend to treat their Mothers. I had to laugh.

About three months into my move into town, my daughter-in-law came over all excited. A local computer business had used school computers for sale for only $100.00 plus a $20.00 fee for a card that would let me get online. It was a good deal, but my money was running low and I had to take care with it. But I really wanted to get online, so said okay, I would do it.

Then I found out it needed a telephone line. My goodness life was complicated on grid.

I so missed the simplicity of my old life.

~ ~ ~

I had lived for a long time with only the most primitive basic needs – shelter, water, oil lamps for light, and wood for warmth. I had added the old cook stove that ran on propane, but that was as much convenience as I knew.

Many times, out of shear habit, I would catch myself thinking of lighting the oil lamps. And it took a long time before I stopped thinking about going to the cistern for drinking water. But here I was, now, with running water and appliances and soon I would have a computer and a phone!

It would take some doing.

While the rest of the world was getting online, I didn't know it existed. Even when cell phones were in their infancy and I got my first monster, it was used very seldom and it was a long process to even get enough bars on it to talk to anyone.

It was a trial by error getting online. At first, I didn't even know my land line would connect me to a service provider. Everyone got a kick out of me. It was all so new, but it was a great thing for me to be able to get online and meet folks.

If you've never known isolation, then you won't understand the feeling of aloneness and how difficult it can be re-entering the human population.

My daughter-in-law was wonderful. Whenever I messed things up on the computer, she would come to help me unscramble it all. It took a while, but finally I got online to *Backwoods Home Magazine* and was able to get email! That was a real shock to me – that communicating with folks so far away could be so easy, nothing more than a little typing.

There, online in the *Backwoods Home Forum*, I would meet and make great friends. Many were curious about my off-grid life. Stranger than the Forum was the chat room, where I could "talk" to people by typing and they could "talk" back. We would laugh and talk about our lives and discuss all the things going on with us.

There were many midnight chats. It seemed I had connected to other humans with the same ideas as my own. Too many times, though, my anger would come out over the loss of my fifty acres. But I did meet a lifelong friend there in an argument about libertarian writer Claire Wolfe. I thought she had said something bad about her but I had misunderstood and we worked it out and to this day, we are fast, true, and devoted friends. Her name in the Forum is LobaAzul aka Lynn.

~ ~ ~

My habits were changing. I seldom went to bed early anymore.

When I lived off-grid, I would read at night by oil lamp but go to bed fairly early, not just to save lamp oil, but because I was tired. Fresh air and lots of physical activity make for early bedtimes.

Now, I would get online, read and write posts on the Backwoods Home Forum and chat with the group who gathered in the live chat room most nights. We talked about chickens and gardens and everything and had cyber-parties which were HI-larious. I really enjoyed that. It sometimes felt strange after being alone for so long, but I really enjoyed my cyber-company.

After one late night session I went to bed with a tropical storm brewing.

~ ~ ~

Trying to make my mobile home more comfortable and nice looking turned out to be a confusing time for me. Every time I thought about what I wanted to do in the mobile home, my mind and heart would jump back to the ole House.

I wanted to fix it up my new home and be comfortable. I needed curtains and a couple of rugs. Sometimes I was like a bull in a china closet. I didn't know which way to go.

I had my 25 gallon propane bottle, so that winter I borrowed a propane space heater to keep warm.

Out of shear vanity, I decided I needed some decent things to wear. And at long last I made a decision to have my hair cut. That took a while as I had to find someone who could cut baby fine hair in the cut I wanted.

Then came the time when my Youngest Son wanted to put a double-wide modular on the lot in front of me. The title for the house and land would be put in his name so they could get financing. I never before made such a big mistake and have lived to regret my decision to this day.

I adored my Son and loved my daughter-in-law as a daughter, but...she had three of the laziest kids ever put on the earth. They wouldn't get up and go to school or, except for one, even stay in school. When they quit, they wouldn't go to work. They would sit around and play video games and stay up all night. The only girl wound up pregnant and broke her stepdad's heart. He wasn't allowed to discipline and it was showing. The youngest boy did manage to graduate, though. That was a miracle, helped along by a very special teacher.

So began a new land survey and construction. New sewer and water lines had to be brought onto the property. A concrete pad was put down for the new modular.

It was a huge, beautiful unit and had all the bells and whistles.

It became a joke in the family that I lived in the "behind" house. My world shrunk. A bunch. Then, they had barely got it on the lot and got moved in when Hurricane Rita decided to make an appearance.

Rita was a huge, bad, ugly hurricane and I would get to test all my skills one more time.

~ ~ ~

The warnings began about a week before Rita hit but I was already prepared. I had plenty of groceries, stores of water, and my oil lamps. The son living in front of me had two generators.

One thing that came in very handy was my Verizon land-line phone. After Rita hit, it would be the only communications outlet for the whole neighborhood. It wasn't a fancy phone, just a plain old one with no bells and whistles which meant it didn't need to be plugged into an electric outlet to work. It ran off the electricity in the phone line so as long as the telephone lines were working, that old phone worked.

We began filling gas cans and gathered the huge coolers we had. We would fill them with ice just before we had to.

The most frustrating part of the preparations involved all the step-kids. They were less than no help. They partied and slept and ran all over the place. Even though they had babies to worry about, they didn't get diapers, baby milk, or baby food. It wasn't like they didn't have the money. They were on welfare. They had plenty of means to prepare. They just couldn't be bothered.

Two days before Rita made landfall, with her 160 to 200 mph winds, the Chief of Police began telling us we had to leave. The day before Rita arrived, a lady Sheriff's deputy came to my door and told me I had to leave right then.

I had to stand my ground and tell her NO!! that I would leave the next morning. We would go to the shelter my son, the lineman, would use. It was built for that very reason.

I have ridden out many storms, but this one was using its main force to come right up our alley and I could tell the winds were not going to be kind.

We finally left six hours before Rita hit and bunked down in the shelter built to withstand up to 200 mph winds.

When the wind started, it literally screamed. Then she hit, with winds so deafening, so powerful, everything shuddered and we could hear the building breathing. The walls seemed so breathe in and out and I understand that was the design.

My Son and I didn't sleep. I wasn't home, we couldn't see out of the building, and didn't know exactly which way she was turning. About 2 a.m., my son and I got up and went to the huge steel doors to check the vehicles. It took both of us to shove the door open. When we got the door open, the wind sucked our breath away. You can't breathe in that kind of wind.

Everything was leaning. Power lines were slapping together making horrible noises.

I am not sure how long she raged, but by daylight we heard a calm, opened the doors, and saw devastation that was unbelievable.

As a lineman, my son was on immediate duty. We gathered bed rolls and gear and loaded up the truck. I had kept the girls in kennels and they were glad to be out.

My Youngest led the way. His big truck had chain saws and much needed emergency equipment. Our little caravan was the only one on the road.

We'd had lots of rain but no flooding. He would stop and clear roads of downed branches and trees. Power lines were all over so we weren't allowed out of our cars. He had all the safety gear of a lineman. He hot-sticked power lines out of the road, cut up bigger limbs, and dragged other limbs and debris out of the road.

Linemen do much more than ride around in trucks. They are the unsung heroes of these horrible storms.

We made the 25-mile trip home in about 2 1/2 hours. As we turned on our street, I almost couldn't look. The fierce winds had torn down huge trees, toppling them like toys. I was afraid my little house would be gone. Thankfully, she wasn't. She was all intact, waiting for me to come home. All those extra 2x4s and hurricane straps made the difference.

My daughter, who had come to stay with us with her hubby and three kids hugged me and said, "Mama it's okay. She made it."

Coffee. That's what I wanted, lots of hot coffee.

A strange effect of hurricanes is that once they're passed, it can become very cool – chilly in fact. Then the heat hit us and it started raining, but that was okay. After surviving the storm, a little rain was nothing.

We fired up one of the propane outdoor cookers and made coffee. My son had to leave us because there were so many power lines down for miles and miles. He would be gone for days.

For weeks following the storm, we had heat index of 116 to about 120 degrees. It was a horrible, oppressive, smothering heat.

We fired up the generators to power the refrigerator, freezer, and fans for the babies. I used power for a few minutes a day to update people on my ole ugly computer. I would log into the *Backwoods Home Forum* to let folks know what was happening. The response and concern for my welfare was unbelievable and to this day I still remember each of them and how much they cared.

Then began weeks of no power, no running water, and heat that could kill you. My Pastor had me checking on folks as I had the only land line working. Travel was limited by law, but I would make ice and water runs in my truck when I could. I also had my little pistol and no fear about using it. I'm glad I never had to.

We had been without electricity for about three weeks, when one morning, as I sat outside early making coffee, I saw three pickup trucks on our little main street. Men were putting on hooks and belts. Linemen!!!

I walked out to see what was going on and got the most awesome feeling. The six of them were from Tennessee and had come in their own trucks to help us. There I stood, a blubbering idiot. They were restoring our lines so when the power was back up we'd have it.

The Army had shown up to help with ice and MREs. (Meals Ready to Eat) They also left armed men at our Chief of Police's disposal.

When the power is out, the gas pumps don't work. For almost two weeks, Our Police Chief had to hand pump gas he had stored into the Patrol cars, but finally it ran out, and he and his men, all three of them, rode four-wheelers to patrol our streets. One looter was shot. We were still under a curfew.

There was no diesel fuel for our huge generator that should be pumping our water to us so we all volunteered to help pass out ice and water. In conversation, it came up that we needed diesel badly. When I got back home, I gave it some thought since I'm usually good in emergency situations. I decided to call Austin. The phone started ringing and kept on ringing until, finally, a man answered. I asked to speak with Governor Perry and he said, "This is Governor Perry."

I almost passed out.

He asked, "How may I help you?" and I told him we were a small community and the bigger towns and cities were getting all the help. We needed diesel fuel for our water pump generator. He asked me where we were and said he'd get on it. Less than eight hours later a truck showed up with the diesel and there I was blubbering again.

Even now, so many years later, I find it astounding it even happened.

~ ~ ~

I loved the jalapeño cheese and crackers, but if you have ever lived on MREs, you know that after a while, though you're not ungrateful for the food, you're just not sure if you can stand it any longer.

Just as I reached that point, the Salvation Army came. A chili dog never tasted so good.

An elderly man and his wife lived at the end of the block. He would bicycle down trying to maintain his balance and carry his to-go plates. I stopped him and told him to just walk down to the house and we'd go together to get our lunch and supper.

If you have any false pride, these catastrophes will break you of the habit. I loved the meals, even the cold sodas, and I didn't usually drink sodas.

As I sat one day eating, I overheard some grumbling about the food, which was mostly chili, the hotdogs, the chicken and dumplings, and stew. I came undone.

"How dare you gripe?" I asked. "What are you doing here? You're getting free hot meals served by folks who say 'God bless you' and are always telling us it'll be okay, and you sit there and gripe about it?"

It made me so upset I stopped by to talk with the Chief. It seemed like he was always up and on top of things, I don't know when he slept. I asked him to please go down and check on the Salvation Army folks, that there were some trouble-makers who were making other folks nervous. He cleaned them out. He later said the gripers didn't even live out here so he politely showed them the city limits.

We emptied the freezer. We had fish fries. I took a roast, dumped it in a big gumbo pot and made a stew. Fast food places that had power were serving what they could get, but mostly they had to throw away millions of dollars-worth of spoiled food.

I was comfortable except for the heat. My years off-grid had kicked in so surviving wasn't going to be a problem for me. I knew how to do this, but I think I was a bit shell-shocked. I wasn't used to people being greedy and hateful. I was used to being alone and making do.

Slowly we got back online. The day the power came on I didn't even know it. I heard the refrigerator running and stood there for a few minutes trying to figure out the noise. Once I did, I plugged in my big fan and went to sleep.

Exhaustion had taken over.

~ ~ ~

Sometimes, it seems like life is in suspended animation. Sometimes, we just put one foot in front of the other.

Cleanup crews showed up, hired by FEMA.

Most folks don't understand these catastrophes. Often, you just can't get emergency services to some areas. You have to clear the roads of downed trees and other debris, opening a trail to get to the people who need you.

Rita tore a path from the Caribbean, across southern Florida and the Gulf to our Texas coast. She hurt us bad but Mississippi folks got hit far worse. I have admired them for a long time. So many lost their homes but you didn't hear them whining. Neighbors pitched in and helped each other.

You live through something like this and it makes you think about these monsters that have no master.

I thought back to nearly freezing to death, to my days of finding a way and making do to survive. All those folks did the same thing. When adversity hits, you gather up the pioneer spirit that is ingrained in each of us and do what you have to do. So many people survived the elements with no power and without roofs on their homes. And winter was coming on. I prayed and cried and felt very helpless for these folks.

As always eventually happens, we slowly got our lives back to normal. True, for many of us, our nerves were shell-shocked – mine the more so from having to worry about and do for family who didn't have a clue nor want one. Why should they? After all, someone was always taking care of them.

I have always known that you cripple people when you do for them what they should be doing for themselves, even if they need to have it forced on them. But it was hard to sit by and do nothing and watch them suffer. I couldn't do it, and my nerves paid the price.

~ ~ ~

I decided I would put up a real Christmas tree with lights this year. I was excited as I dug out my homemade decorations. At night I would sit and look at the beautiful lights and shininess of it all and I would cry.

My old way of celebrating Christmas was almost holy to me. I'd go out and cut a scraggly pine or a holly and decorate it with some homemade things. It wasn't much, but there was sense of accomplishment in it, and a feeling of peace at night when I sat and looked at it. Now, all I had to do was plug in the lights.

I had long since quit buying gifts for people. Two weeks after Christmas, no one remembered what you gave them anyway. Instead, I baked, and kept the cookies going and that they remembered. They still do, to this day.

I'd been keeping in touch occasionally with The Postman. One night the phone rang and it was his son, The Ego. He told me his father had a heart attack and stroke. He told me they searched for my number because they knew I would want to know what happened. After a few minutes of casual conversation, I was asked if I would come take care of him. I should have figured there was a selfish reason for him to have called.

I had to say no. I would never go to Hopewell Road again. To my mind, it was his kids' responsibility to care for him.

I don't know how long he lasted, but I know where he rests – in a little burial ground called Mustang Cemetery out on Gate Road.

That winter was very cold. It is many times after hurricanes. And that feeling of discontent and anxiety came back, a feeling of fear that something wasn't right. I should not have thrown that problems list away.

~ ~ ~

Over the winter, we got back to a normal routine. I had my spare room set up with my sewing machine and I wanted to make some aprons. Many of the apron patterns I found were either too skimpy or short, so I altered one. It's all taped together now, but to this day, I still use that same one.

One of the members of the *Backwoods Home Forum* posted a garden thread on hay bale gardening. I had never heard of growing things in hay! That spring I grew some peas in a bale of horse hay. I had potted plants all over my little porch and in front of the mobile home. I wished I could have planted more, but my yard had gotten so small now that there were so many cars and people.

I had found some heavy curtains at a garage sale, altered them, and put them up, which gave me a bit of privacy. Privacy became a big issue as the family moved into the modular.

~ ~ ~

The crowd of people in and out of my house all day and night got to be a bit much. But since I was step-grandma, I had no rights.

As bad was the way the yard was treated. Trash was thrown in the yard. Baby diapers thrown at (not in) the trash cans we had set up.

It got to where I was picking up soda cans and candy wrappers and disposable diapers and hauling six to eight trash cans to the dump once or twice a week. I finally had to say something. I knew the kids were spoiled brats and I would be the bad guy regardless of my actions. Slamming doors and loud talking would bring me straight out of bed.

Line breaks from storms were the norm, so my Youngest Son was out on calls all the time. His absence caused a great many problems, especially with the kids. I say kids, but they were not small. They were grown and with him gone all the time, they had nobody to discipline them and teach them.

The welfare debit card spent most of its time at the local fast food place.

I tried to rock along but it was difficult. I kept thinking about moving the mobile home again, but it was almost impossible with the huge modular in front of me.

Summer was so hot and I was broke. Literally broke. I got a job at Walmart on the night shift, which saved me, but it couldn't make up for all the money I had spent.

~ ~ ~

I tried everything to sleep. After working nights I would come in and take care of my girls, Tippy and Sammy. About the time I wanted go to bed for the day, they'd be getting up.

And so it began. A huge fight was brewing and I would lose.

I didn't have any problems with my daughter-in-law but she wasn't willing to discipline and her now-adult kids knew it. Time and again she'd give in to her overbearing brats just to keep the peace.

As bad as it was then, I didn't know that the expense of a huge wedding my step-grandson wanted, coupled with other problems, would cause the greatest family rift I would ever know.

It was coming and I didn't have a clue.

~ ~ ~

I had put all the money I had in my new home and the job at Walmart wasn't bring in enough, so I applied early for my Social Security. I would take a penalty for it but I needed to regroup. It wasn't much money but it would keep me going after getting the shock of my life.

Two weeks before my birthday, a year after Hurricane Rita, a Deputy knocked on my door. I thought something had happened to one of the family.

No. It was an order of eviction and to appear before the local Justice of the Peace.

I was stunned. I got sick to my stomach. I couldn't speak. I couldn't move a muscle.

~ ~ ~

My Son was on the road working. I went over to my daughter-in-law and asked her what was up. She was pale and shaking. We couldn't talk.

It turned out that the financing of the huge modular required the title to the land and they had not been making their mortgage payments.

(Lesson: NEVER use land as collateral to build/buy a house. Don't do it. Ever.)

I had no idea that everything on the land was subject to the loan I thought it was just their house. Nor did I know my house was considered a "storage unit." What?

The idea of losing my home again upset me so much I barely managed to go to work. I couldn't eat and lost weight quickly. I shook and had such anxiety attacks I was taking Benadryl to calm them.

The day of going to court came. I didn't have money for a lawyer, but I sure needed one.

No matter what I said, nor how I pleaded, the Justice wouldn't listen to me. I even offered to buy back my mobile home/storage shed but he said no and gave us all six days to move.

I had to appeal to his human side. I told him I worked nights at Walmart and I needed time to gather money and find a place to live.

He thought about it and finally gave me two weeks.

When I came home after court with my Son in his truck right behind me, my daughter-in-law stepped out the door of the house and asked me how it went.

I told her we had lost and had to move.

Her only words to me until this day about the whole affair were, "They can't do that."

I turned to her and said, "Well HE just did."

It was September 11, my sixty-fifth birthday.

Since Hurricane Rita, there were few rentals available. There were so many properties with their roofs gone or that had been condemned.

Two days before time ran out, I found a horrible old house. The windows were knocked out of one bedroom and the kitchen sink emptied onto the ground. The hurricane had pulled it apart and it was impossible to cool and by the first of November I would find out how cold it could get. Add to that, it wasn't a very safe place to live.

After working all night, I woke up one day to my girls barking their heads off at a man standing in the living room. I grabbed my Mossberg and asked him if he knew he was going to die. He was high, and told me he had come for the rent. He was the landlord's step-son and had gotten a key and just come in.

My rent was already paid.

I had to find something else.

~ ~ ~

I knew I had to move.

I called my Daughter and told her to look for a small RV or something. I gave notice at Walmart because I couldn't function and work. I started putting all my stuff in a small storage place in town.

I was worn out and mentally on the edge of losing my mind. Hate and anger and the sheer feeling of being whipped began to take over. Thankfully, my dear Daughter called and told me a friend had an old job shack – an RV-type trailer – I could buy for a hundred dollars. I told her I was on my way.

It was a trashed out mess but she said the friend's boys would clean it out and her hubby would move it.

If you think you can't lose your mind, that life is doable at all times, think again. I was very close.

My Daughter and son-in-law told me they would set up the shack on their little place. With three kids of their own, they didn't have room for me in their house.

Rita had taken a lot of their roof. They tried to get help but to no avail so Son-in-law had patched as best he could. He was a returning Veteran and was making very little money.

So would begin another recovery.

But not before I had to wrestle with my demons.

~ ~ ~

Just as we set up the little job shack, a bad blue-norther hit.

I had taken only the basics. I hooked up the propane heater and we had to block a window that was broken out. We were able to run a power cord from their house, so I had electricity, but no water or sewer or way to cook.

That night I put the girls in bed with me. The temperature dropped to freezing and the wind blew.

Nights in the ole House were as cold as this, but never felt like this. This was a painful cold. My mind raged and my soul was hurt.

The next morning, I went over and made coffee at my daughter's house. To this day, I don't remember when I stopped crying. Suddenly, I didn't have an Internet connection and had only my old, prepaid cell phone.

My daughter let me get online on her computer.

Then began the "you'll go to my church if you live" here dance.

~ ~ ~

The norther passed and it warmed up a bit. I had to get some order going.

We had walled up the doorway to the back room. The roof was in bad shape there and the floor was gone.

I had to have some way to wash up so I got my water hose and

187

hooked it from the house to the RV. The bathrooms in my daughter's house were almost non-functional.

I had a little kitchen area but nothing else; no stove or refrigerator.

I was in a pit, one I couldn't find a way to get out of.

~ ~ ~

Winter was so cold. I wasn't eating well and the stress of being held captive by the situation took its toll on me.

My Daughter was in superior mode. She had gotten the religion bug and was so over-bearing in her zeal. She had no idea she wasn't appointed by God over me, that she wasn't superior. Her preaching just made things worse.

The winter months drug by. I was able to get online to the *Backwoods Home Forum* when my daughter was gone.

My friends there saw I was in serious trouble. They sent letters and one lady sent me a microwave so I could cook. Another would come to be able to read my desperation in my posts and chats. If not for their gentle care and concern, I would be dead or homeless or worse – totally insane.

I got a job in a daycare where my Daughter worked and although the pay was low, it worked for me. It got me out of the house and focused on something other than my problems for a few hours each workday.

Of course, that was the time the fuel injection system in my truck began to pitch a fit. I would barely make it back and forth to the daycare. One of the ladies from the Forum loaned me the money to get it fixed. Two months later the twin catalytic converters went out.

I was totally at the mercy of everything and everyone.

I was in the newborn/creeper nursery at the daycare and the babies caught a virus, so the doors had to be kept closed for their safety and as a precaution against infecting the older children as well as for the babies' protection. Naturally, I caught one of their colds.

By then, my Daughter had quit the nursery. My truck was down and I had no ride and now I was sick. I curled up in a ball. I didn't know how to function anymore.

~ ~ ~

My Youngest Son, who had lost the place we lived, came by to check on me. He had bought another house using money from his 401k he borrowed against. That would stick in my craw for years, knowing he had access to money that could have saved both of our homes.

He knew I was in dire straits and that my health was in seriously jeopardy. I didn't have a mirror to look at so I couldn't see how bad I was.

He told me to grab some clothes and the dogs and go home with him for a few days. It turned out to be a new day.

I began to eat properly and had one little check coming from the last of the lawsuit.

My Son hauled my truck to a friend of his that did converter work and all the exhaust system for a big company. I had previous estimates on fixing my truck that ran from $1200 to $1400, but that amount was impossible for me.

When my Son told him it was his mother's truck, the young man told him that he would fix it for $425. I know I must have looked astounded when I asked him why and how he could do it that cheap. He said he knew where there was a wrecked truck and he could buy the converters for $400.00 and would charge me $25.00 labor.

He didn't know how it took everything I had not to cry hysterically with thankfulness and joy.

Then he said, "You remind me of my Mother." She recently passed away and he hoped someone would show her the same compassion if she was still alive. I will leave it to you folks to mull that over.

One simple act of kindness – you never know when or how it will affect someone. It certainly affected me.

I was feeling a lot better a week later when the fellow called and told me my truck was ready. I told him I didn't have my little check yet to pay him. He told me to come get my truck and pay him when the check arrived.

Once I had my truck again, I moved all my things to a little camper on my Son's place. Then I got organized.

I took care of my precious girls. They both were aging fast. Life had not been kind to them as they followed me around, but they never failed to be there when I came home from work in my last years with them. I do believe they kept me alive many times because they were there and looked to me to take care of them.

I reapplied at Walmart and they hired me back on. I worked another almost six years for them.

My Life Now

My Oldest Son completed his sentence and parole and returned to Texas. He gave me money to buy a small house that is free and clear of debt. It was a blessing I didn't expect, but dealing with aging and with getting him settled after many years of being away from the family required a lot of emotional adjustment that took its toll on me.

My Middle Son married a cancer survivor and they are each other's guardian angels.

My Youngest Son has been doing much better. He and my daughter-in-law continue to be married. After many separations and counseling they are working it all out.

Although I have made peace with them, I have moments of flashback hate over the unnecessary loss of my home and other issues. I am human after all. But I have too much love for my family, warts and all, to let bad feelings linger.

I think many parents can identify with that. And as human beings, we have to learn not to set ourselves up in such perfect worlds. Life *isn't* perfect and expecting it to remain so for long is just asking for heartache and disappointment.

In the end, I was gifted with a computer from a lady I cared for after I retired from Walmart. Once again, I could regularly connect with the people of the *Backwoods Home Forum* and *The Gulch*. So many are friends who didn't give up on me even when I was close to giving up on myself. They were and are wonderful people who never stopped sharing their love and encouragement.

~ ~ ~

Is this the end of my story? Yes and No.

Each day I try to pay back by encouraging and propping up folks who need it. Each time the north winds of winter blow, my mind goes back to a simpler time in my life; to an ole House that sheltered me and taught me; to the joy of discovering I could do it, *whatever* it was.

Of course, the greatest gifts of all are the dear friends who are still there in the Forums. Sadly, we have lost so many, Preliator and Melonghunter among them. They were two very tall men and we'll always miss them. But we carry their memories.

Then there are the ladies who still carry on – Lynn, Bama Suzy, Nancy, and many, many more who call me friend and who are continued blessings.

My words of wisdom:

Never Back Up Nor Quit.

Regroup, Adapt and Overcome.

Always remember – Trouble Rides a Fast Horse.

Sometimes it's a very fast, dark one at that, but without the dark we wouldn't know the blessing of the beautiful Sunlight of The Spirit.

I have added grandchildren and great-grandchildren.

I had to have ole Tippy put down in her 17th year. Sammy went two years later. Both were the last parts of an off-grid life I had lived and loved and will miss until the day I close my eyes for the last time.

I am so grateful for the chance at a self-reliant life. If not for it, where would I be? What would I have missed? Life – I would have missed life.

Sometimes, it's been a strain, sometimes it's been very harsh, and sometimes it's been heartbreaking. But many times, it's been joyous and peaceful.

And I can live with that.

Thank you for reading this small story of my life off-grid and beyond.

Humbly,

Annie

A Widow's Walk Off-Grid to Self-Reliance is also available in large print and for Kindle readers and apps

For more information, please visit www.masonmarshall.com.